IMPACT:

Pentecost and the Early Church

Also by Peter Wade:

For a current list of books,
visit https://www.PeterWade.com/books/

IMPACT

Pentecost and the Early Church

PETER WADE

POSITIVE
WORD
MINISTRIES

Published by Positive Word Ministries Inc.,
39 Schooner Road, Seaford SA 5169, Australia
https://www.PeterWade.com

ISBN: 978-0-909362-57-7
Version 1.2
Cover photo: © Pentecost by Mark Wiggin
www.markwigginart.com

I am aware of the Greek words *pneuma hagion*, "holy spirit," with and without the Greek article, and generally accept the distinction. However, the usage or non-usage of the article to show the Giver or the gift and operations is not consistent, and requires the context. No major English translation reflects this difference, and only three of the others attempt to show it: the Concordant Literal NT and the Mirror Bible in the text, and the Companion Bible in the side-notes and Appendix 101. The author has therefore continued using the traditional capitals for the convenience of the majority of readers.

A few chapters have been edited from the Positive Words email newsletter. Website addresses given are correct at the time of publication.

Bible Abbreviations Used

AMP	The Amplified Bible
ASV	American Standard Version (1901)
CEV	Contemporary English Version
CSB	Holman Christian Standard Bible
ESV	English Standard Version
GNB	Good News Bible
KJV	King James Version
MIRROR	The Mirror Bible
MOFFATT	The New Testament: A New Translation
MSG	The Message Bible
NASB	New American Standard Bible
NET	New English Bible
NIV	New International Version
NKJV	New King James Version
NLT	New Living Translation
WUEST	The New Testament: An Expanded Translation

Contents

First Words

In the first verse of the book of Acts we read, *"In the first book, O Theophilus, I have dealt with all that Jesus began to do and teach."* So the book of the Acts of the Apostles is a sequel to another work by the same writer. Luke's gospel in its prologue reads: *"³It seemed good to me also, having followed all things closely for some time past, to write an orderly account for you, most excellent Theophilus, ⁴that you may have certainty concerning the things you have been taught" (Luke 1:3-4).* Attempts to identify Theophilus appear to have been unsuccessful, but the "most excellent" indicates a high official.

As one Bible teacher has written: "Acts was written by Luke between 63 and 65 A.D. It is a history of the first thirty-three years of Christ as the right hand of the Father. It is a sample of the supernatural life of the sons of God carrying out the will of their seated Lord... There isn't a thing that Jesus did in His earth walk that the Name [of Jesus] will not do today in the lips of the New Creation" (E.W. Kenyon, *Advanced Bible Course,* Lesson 27).

I want to focus on the first six chapters, which cover the first two years or so of the early church, though it is difficult to be accurate. The apostles were suddenly "thrown in at the deep end" having witnessed the death of their leader, then his resurrection, and on the day of ascension the command to stay in the city until they received power from on high. They knew something was going to happen but they had few details. Ten days after the Ascension of Jesus came the Day of Pentecost and all the incredible events that followed.

My viewpoint is based on the solid foundation that the Bible as originally written within the vocabulary of the writer is the "God-breathed" Word of God (II Timothy 3:16). *"Given by inspiration of God"* (KJV) is one word in the Greek, *theopneustos.*

In its application to Luke-Acts, that belief is not concerned with theories such as the "we" in the narrative "signifies others keeping a diary during the Acts period and sharing them with Luke." If the two narrative accounts by Luke are "God inspired," then they are as acceptable of a source of theology as Paul's letters. Out of this stance, I believe there is no great divide between theology and narrative, and narrative becomes a record of people living out a theology, either consciously or otherwise. This work, therefore, is not an academic thesis but a practical recounting of the events with application to believers today.*

---

* For an academic discussion, I would recommend *The Charismatic Theology of St. Luke* by Roger Stronstad (1984; second edition 2012, Baker).

1

From Sad to Satisfied!

The first eleven verses of Acts chapter 1 recount selected events in the life of Christ following his resurrection, detailing activities of the apostles and other believers after his ascension. *"I have dealt with all that Jesus began to do and teach, ²until the day when he was taken up, after he had given commands through the Holy Spirit to the apostles whom he had chosen"* (Acts 1:1b-2).

Not every event is mentioned, and there is one in Luke chapter 24 that I would like to comment on as a bridge to Luke's record in Acts. It took place on Resurrection Day. Just about every preacher would love to have been there, or at least been a fly on the wall and overheard the conversation. A complete account is given in Luke 24:13-25. *"¹³That very day two of them were going to a village named Emmaus, about seven miles [11 km] from Jerusalem, ¹⁴and they were talking with each other about all these things that had happened"* (verses 13-14). "They were deep in conversation..." (MSG), "they communed" (ASV) and reasoned, as the Greek text uses a different word from "talking" or "speaking." "This term suggests emotional dialogue and can thus be translated 'debated'" (NET).

Like so many events recorded in the Bible, this "God moment" took place during an activity common to everyday life. Two disciples were walking down a road leaving Jerusalem on their way home and while they walked a conversation took place. For the record, only one disciple is named, Cleopas (verse 18), and he was not one of the twelve nor is he mentioned elsewhere in the New Testament.

"While they were talking and discussing together, Jesus himself drew near and went with them. [16]But their eyes were kept from recognizing him" (verses 15-16). The same incident in Mark 16:12 states that Jesus was "in another form," and no one really knows what that means. The important point is at the moment they were aware of a companion, these disciples thought he was a stranger.

"And he said to them, 'What is this conversation that you are holding with each other as you walk?' And they stood still, looking sad. [18]Then one of them, named Cleopas, answered him, 'Are you the only visitor to Jerusalem who does not know the things that have happened there in these days?'" (verses 17-18). Now it is about to get interesting. Two disciples, their sadness at the events of the past few days clearly evident, and the Jesus they had watched being crucified standing next to them in their sadness.

Oh, how I wish I was a great orator. I'd really set the house on fire with verse 17! Haldor Lillenas (1885-1959) wrote a hymn on this incident:

> One is walking with me over life's uneven way,
> Constantly supporting me each moment of the day.
> How can I be lonely when such fellowship is mine,
> With my blessed Lord divine!

Just think about it for a moment; it is even greater

than the lyrics suggest. We have *"Christ in you, the hope of glory"* (Colossians 1:27), and that spirit reality should change your sadness, the problems you face, the needs you have. It is a great picture to see him walking alongside his disciples, but in the church age we have him *in* us. So wherever we go Christ is there too!

*"And he said to them, 'What things?' And they said to him, 'Concerning Jesus of Nazareth, a man who was a prophet mighty in deed and word before God and all the people, *[20]*and how our chief priests and rulers delivered him up to be condemned to death, and crucified him. *[21]*But we had hoped that he was the one to redeem Israel. Yes, and besides all this, it is now the third day since these things happened'"* (verses 19-21). "We had hoped..." but that redemption doesn't seem possible now that he's dead, so there is the source of their sadness.

And further add to the confusion to their hopes, *"Moreover, some women of our company amazed us. They were at the tomb early in the morning, *[23]*and when they did not find his body, they came back saying that they had even seen a vision of angels, who said that he was alive. *[24]*Some of those who were with us went to the tomb and found it just as the women had said, but him they did not see"* (verses 22-24). In other words, we don't know what to believe!

*"[25]And he said to them, 'O foolish ones, and slow of heart to believe all that the prophets have spoken! *[26]*Was it not necessary that the Christ should suffer these things and enter into his glory?' *[27]*And beginning with Moses and all the Prophets, he interpreted to them in all the Scriptures the things concerning himself"* (verses 25-27). "Foolish

ones" is from a common word meaning "without sense." Today a paraphrased version could probably say, "Dumb and Dumber!" The Amplified Bible adds "[sluggish in mind, dull of perception]." Jesus had said they were also "slow of heart"; that is, "with hearts so slow to believe, after all the prophets have declared!" (Moffatt).

They could be forgiven for being sad, but there was no excuse for not believing what the Jewish prophets had written concerning the coming Messiah. "Man's basic spiritual problem is the integrity of God's Word," as I have constantly quoted one teacher. The problem remains to this day. And until you settle that question you will never find satisfaction in Christ. Since God said what He meant, and meant what He said, then you have the simple joy of believing it. This is not religion, it is reality.

How every preacher would like to have Jesus' commentary from Moses onward through all the prophets, of all that was written concerning him! Yet we do have many truths regarding this in Paul's revelation and its application today to Christian believers on the other side of the cross.

"*28So they drew near to the village to which they were going. He acted as if he were going farther, 29but they urged him strongly, saying, 'Stay with us, for it is toward evening and the day is now far spent.' So he went in to stay with them. 30When he was at table with them, he took the bread and blessed and broke it and gave it to them. 31And their eyes were opened, and they recognized him. And he vanished from their sight. 32They said to each other, 'Did not our hearts burn [glow, Moffatt] within us while he talked to us on the road, while he opened to us the Scriptures?'"* (verses 28-32).

Here is the heart of the account, as well as the key to how you, as a believer, can have the glow also. It was not the words that Jesus spoke, nor the way he delivered them, that brought the glow—it was **the Scriptures being opened,** shown how they fit together, *"as he* [the master Teacher] *talked to us on the road."* The word for "opened" is the same word used in verse 31 of their eyes being opened. So many Christians miss the "glow" that comes from an authentic understanding of God's Word. The Bible is not a dull book that has to be read religiously every day. It is the food that sustains the believer every moment. *"Man shall not live by bread alone, but by every word that comes from the mouth of God"* (Matthew 4:4). May this book help bring the glow into your life.

"Ah! this accounts for it: We could not understand the glow of self-evidencing light, love, glory that ravished our hearts; but now we do" (JFB Commentary). Yet now we have something even better and the glow should brighten to intensity of light! *"But when the Helper comes, whom I will send to you from the Father, the Spirit of truth, who proceeds from the Father, he will bear witness about me, 27And you also will bear witness, because you have been with me from the beginning"* (John 15:26-27). The Helper, the Comforter, came on the Day of Pentecost, and he does bear witness of the Christ within and the mind of Christ within. I will look at this deeper in Chapter 6.

2

Wait! There's More

In the 40 days between the Resurrection and Ascension of Jesus, there are records of many witnesses to the facts. Let's look at a few moments of this period when the resurrected Christ walked on this earth.

"He presented himself alive to them after his suffering by many proofs, appearing to them during forty days and speaking about the kingdom of God" (Acts 1:3). On one occasion He appeared to over 500 believers at one time (I Corinthians 15:6), and to the disciples both individually and collectively many times.

In Luke 24:30-48 (same event as John 20:19-25), Jesus appeared to all his disciples (except Thomas), *"Then he opened their minds to understand the Scriptures, [46]and said to them, 'Thus it is written, that the Christ should suffer and on the third day rise from the dead, [47]and that repentance and forgiveness of sins should be proclaimed in his name to all nations, beginning from Jerusalem. [48]You are witnesses of these things. [49]And behold, I am sending the promise of my Father upon you. But **stay** in the city **until** you are clothed with power from on high.'"* (Luke

24:45-49 ESV).

"Tarry ye in the city of Jerusalem, until ye be endued with power from on high" (verse 49 KJV).

This is the "Wait! There's more." He had spoken about this promise before. In John 7:38-39 in that famous incident in the temple on the last day of the feast, Jesus alluded to the coming Pentecost, *"'Whoever believes in me, as the Scripture has said, "Out of his heart will flow rivers of living water."' ³⁹Now this he said about the Spirit, whom those who believed in him were to receive, for as yet the Spirit had not been given, because Jesus was not yet glorified"* (ESV).

Then on the night before Jesus was killed, he told his disciples clearly, *"Nevertheless, I tell you the truth: it is to your advantage that I go away, for if I do not go away, the Helper will not come to you. But if I go, I will send him to you"* (John 16:7). So it should have been no surprise to be told to "stay in the city until you are clothed with power from on high." Then in Acts 1:4-5 Luke states: *"And while staying with them he ordered them **not** to depart from Jerusalem, but to **wait** for the promise of the Father, which, he said, 'you heard from me; ⁵for John baptized with water, but you will be baptized with [in] the Holy Spirit not many days from now.'"*

The Azusa Street Pentecostal revival of 1906 (which came out of the holiness movement of the 1800s) took this command to tarry as being applicable to all believers in Christ for all time. Pentecostal churches held "tarrying meetings" where they would pray and plead to be baptized with the Holy Spirit, the Helper, the Comforter, the giver of power from on high (Acts 1:8). However, the command was obviously given at the Ascension only to the eleven remaining disciples to stay in Jerusalem, the city where they were when Jesus gave the instruction.

Preachers do not need to see the command as figurative, such as "**your** Jerusalem, the city where you live," but should accept the narrative as literal. *"Wait for... not many days from now"* (verse 5). And that is what they did for however long it took, which was 10 days after the Ascension. No-one appears to have waited again in the records of the book of Acts. Once other believers knew the promise was activated, they received the gift without tarrying.

We should also note that after the Day of Pentecost, the term "baptized" was used only once in relation to the Holy Spirit (Acts 11:6) and that was a quotation of the promise given in Acts 1:5. All other references in Acts are to John's ritual of baptism in water for new converts. "The basic act of receiving the spirit can be described as being baptized or filled, but the verb 'baptize' is not used for subsequent experiences. *Footnote:* The noun-phrase 'baptism in the Holy Spirit' does not occur in the NT" (Tyndale New Testament Commentary, 2008) but "baptized with the Holy Spirit" is used in Acts 11:16. Both phrases are, however, common among Pentecostals and Charismatics. In Acts 2:38 Peter renamed the experience *"the gift of the Holy Spirit,"* and that term appears in Acts chapters 8, 10 and 11.

You don't have to "tarry" or "stay in the city," for just as Christ died *"once for all"* (Romans 6:10), so the Holy Spirit was given once to include all believers for the entire church age. You don't have to beg and plead, you just need to accept the gift. *"11What father among you, if his son asks for a fish, will instead of a fish give him a serpent;* [12]*or if he asks for an egg, will give him a scorpion?* [13]*If you then, who are evil, know how to give good gifts to your children, how much more will the heavenly Father give the Holy Spirit to those who ask him"* (Luke 11:11-13).

"Pentecost" is the Greek word for "the fiftieth day" and refers to 50 days after the Passover, when the Jewish people held the Feast of the Harvest. The Acts 2 occasion of Pentecost was a once-only historical event that ushered in a replacement for the old Jewish religion. The Church Universal is under the headship of the resurrected Christ, who now sits on the right hand of the Father's throne. The Book of Acts is the history of the first 33 years of the early church as they followed the instructions of ascended Christ by the power of the Spirit within them to share the good news with the then known world.

Whenever they needed help it was available by revelation, including how to fix their mistakes, where to go next, what to say in front of rulers, and how to encourage one another in the outworking of the spirit within. You and I also have that same Helper, Comforter, who is resident within us, and we should listen to his guidance and use his power to meet the needs of people the Father sends across our paths.

3

The Power of Pentecost

In the last chapter I referred to the verses that gave the promise of Pentecost, and it is important that I give some emphasis to the continual use of the word "power" in those promises. The Greek word translated "power" is *dunamis* and appears 120 times in the New Testament, sometimes translated as "might, strength or ability."

There is a different Greek word for the power that comes from authority (*exousia*), which in modern versions is translated as "authority." *Dunamis* has come into the English language as "dynamic" and "dynamo," and later the word "dynamite" was coined by the inventor Alfred Nobel in 1867. "Dynamo" has been supplanted by the word "generator," for that is what it does; it generates power. As a young teenager I had what was called a dynamo. It generated power for the lights on my bicycle by means of a serrated wheel that ran on the side of the front tire.

For the sake of completeness, the KJV translates *ischus* as "power" in II Thessalonians 1:9. Other translations prefer force or strength. *Kratos* is translated "power" four times, and *energes* (compare the English "energetic") three times. In this book I will concentrate on *dunamis*.

So many people think that unless God sends lightning bolts as He thunders from on high, then God's power is not at work. While there are Bible examples of God getting people's attention that way, they are few and far between. God's command to His people is the exact opposite: *"Be still, and know that I am God"* (Psalm 46:10).

Unfortunately many Pentecostals and Charismatics ignore this, thinking noise is power, yet they want their car to move as quiet as a mouse! I recall one occasion when a combined Pentecostal meeting was being held in a public hall in North Perth, Western Australia. When Vivien and I entered through the front door, we could hear the noise of pastors' praying in a back room behind the stage. They had arranged for a messenger to invite Pastor Wade to join them when I arrived, but I replied, "I think they are doing alright without my contribution!"

I view God's power that is within every spirit-filled Christian as latent power, something that is capable of becoming active or at hand but has not yet achieved that state. I have often used the illustration of a car battery. That rectangular object sitting next to the engine has latent power. When you start the engine by turning the key in the lock or pressing a button, the power resident in the battery is released and the engine starts. At that point the power becomes live or actual.

The power in a car battery is also undesignated power, because it is the same power that unlocks the door of the car when I press a button on the remote. It is also the same power that runs the GPS map, the audio, the lights, the turn signals, and whatever else has been built into the cabin of the vehicle.

Likewise, the power line coming into my house is undesignated. Once the power line has entered the meter on the wall, it gets divided by cables for lighting and another cable for power. The power cable is further divided to work the air-conditioner, the television, the electric kettle, and the computers and telephones, etc.

On the Day of Pentecost, the power of God was first manifested as *"a sound like a mighty rushing wind"* (Acts 2:2). Then *"divided tongues as of fire appeared to them and rested on each one of them"* (verse 3), and they *"began to speak in other tongues [languages]"* (verse 4). Peter stood up and activated that power to witness to the death and resurrection of Jesus and to call for repentance so that the listeners also could *"receive the gift of the Holy Spirit"* (verses 14-40).

The power of God is often voice-activated, which means it is faith-activated and we believe it strong enough to speak it out. In chapter 3 we see it displayed as power to heal the lame beggar, and open the way for Peter to yet again employ the power to witness to the assembled crowd. He was arrested and the next day had to face the High Priest who wanted to know *"By what power or by what name did you do this?"* (Acts 4:7) And so we could continue on through the book of Acts.

In the Bible, the power of God is at work in many other situations beside witnessing and healing. The power that is resident in the believer is equal to the power that raised Christ from the dead: *"[19]The immeasurable greatness of his power toward us who believe, according to the working of his great might [20]that he worked in Christ when he raised him from the dead and seated him at his right hand in the heavenly places"* (Ephesians 1:19-20). Now that is power!

"The gospel... is the power of God for salvation to everyone who believes..." (Romans 1:16). The gospel or good news is how we know that God has provided salvation for us. *"Faith comes from hearing, and hearing through the word of Christ"* (Romans 10:17). So, unless we hear the gospel, we will not be saved. In Paul's testimony to King Agrippa, he recounted what Jesus said to him on the road to Damascus: *"I am sending you* [18]*to open their eyes, so that they may turn from darkness to light and from the power of Satan to God, that they may receive forgiveness of sins and a place among those who are sanctified by faith in me"* (Acts 26:17b-18).

Another manifestation of power is wealth. God warned His people in the Old Testament, *"Beware lest you say in your heart, 'My power and the might of my hand have gotten me this wealth...'* [18]*You shall remember the Lord your God, for it is he who gives you power to get wealth"* (Deuteronomy 8:17-18a). This truth is also stated in Ecclesiastes 5:19: *"Everyone also to whom God has given wealth and possessions and power to enjoy them, and to accept his lot and rejoice in his toil—this is the gift of God."* According to one author, Jesus spoke considerably more about money (2,000+ times) than he did about faith (246 times) and love (733 times)! With this solid biblical foundation, many of the prominent Pentecostal evangelists preach prosperity as well as healing of the body.

In the Christian life, we are kept (KJV) or guarded by God's power. *"Who [the believers] by God's power are being guarded through faith for a salvation ready to be revealed in the last time"* (I Peter 1:5). *"But the Lord is faithful. He will establish you and guard you against the evil one"* (II Thessalonians 3:3). In fact, everything we need for whatever we will run across comes by the power of God: *"His divine power has granted to us all things that pertain to life and godliness, through the knowledge of him who called us to his own glory and excellence"* (II Peter 1:3).

In God's church, a minister is not someone who has completed special studies at college level and is then recognized by a denomination. In the Church age, he or she is like Paul: *"Of this gospel I was made a minister according to the gift of God's grace, which was given me by the working of his power"* (Ephesians 3:7). Made a minister by the working of God's power and grace. Not by a college!

Finally, Paul sums it up beautifully in Ephesians 3:20: *"Now to him who is able to do far more abundantly than all that we ask or think, according to the power at work within us."* The power of God within you can do far more than you can even dare to imagine.

4

The First Business Meeting

Myles Coverdale, in his 1535 translation of the Bible, wrote: "It shall greatly helpe ye to understand Scripture, if thou mark not only what is spoken or wrythen, but of whom and to whom, with what words, at what time, where, to what intent, with what circumstances, considering what goeth before and what followeth."

So I shall apply his exhortation as we move on in Acts chapter 1. After the Ascension of Jesus in Acts 1:9, the apostles *"returned to Jerusalem from the mount called Olivet, which is near Jerusalem, a Sabbath day's journey away. [13]And when they had entered, they went up to the upper room, **where they were staying**, Peter and John and James and Andrew, Philip and Thomas, Bartholomew and Matthew, James the son of Alphaeus and Simon the Zealot and Judas the son of James"* (Acts 1:12-13). Luke records that they *"returned to Jerusalem with great joy, [53]and were continually in the temple blessing God"* (Luke 24:52a-53).

We discover here that the eleven were staying in "the upper room." This term has become forever associated with Pentecost, mentioned in many Christian hymns and songs and books, and from 1935 onward is the name of a widely-read daily devotional magazine.

Early in my ministry as a denominational Pentecostal pastor I remember preaching a sermon on "Seven Steps to the Upper Room." I gave seven actions that should be performed to receive the gift of the Spirit. While I preached some good homiletic sermons in those early years, this was not one of them and I'm sure I never used the outline again (which would have been a "re-bore" as one preacher's son described a recycled sermon!) The denomination's belief was to have "tarrying meetings" to receive "the baptism of the Spirit," but we have seen already why these meetings are not necessary.

"These all continued with one accord in prayer and supplication, with the women and Mary the mother of Jesus, and with His brothers" (Acts 1:14 NKJV). The "continued" word needs to be seen in the light of Luke 24:53, Acts 2:46 and 3:1, indicating that as Jews they would go to the temple for the three regular hours of prayer. They also gathered with other Christians in their homes for prayers (Acts 4:23), especially when there was persecution or needs that were to be met.

The rest of Acts chapter 1 records the first business meeting of the church, as there was a vacancy following the suicide of Judas Iscariot. *"In those days Peter stood up among the brothers (the company of persons was in all about 120)..."* (Acts 1:15). Peter seems to have taken the role of leader, undoubtedly by mutual consent.

The qualifications of the replacement was stated: *"[21] So one of the men who have accompanied us during all the time that the Lord Jesus went in and out among us,*

[22]beginning from the baptism of John until the day when he was taken up from us—one of these men must become with us a witness to his resurrection.' [23]*And they put forward two, Joseph called Barsabbas, who was also called Justus, and Matthias"* (Acts 1:21-23). Two nominations were made. Prayer followed for God to guide their voting, *"And they cast lots for them, and the lot fell on Matthias, and he was numbered with the eleven apostles"* (Acts 1:26). Casting lots was the Jewish method of voting, *"The lot is cast into the lap, but its every decision is from the Lord"* (Proverbs 16:33; see also 18:18). Matthias is not mentioned again in the New Testament. And by simple math, eleven plus one equals twelve! Please remember that.

5

The Participants and
the Place

Moving on to Acts 2:1 we come to the "who" and the "where." *"[And] when the day of Pentecost arrived, **they were** all together in one **place**."* Many modern translations omit words to conform with current English style. The Greek word for "and" is present in the text, but the ESV, NIV, NKJV, CSB, etc., omit the conjuction "and" at the start of verse 1. This adds to the confusion in reading what is written in this verse.

Let's take the word "they" first. It is a third person plural subject pronoun and is used of a group of people. So reading back before its use, we discover two groups of people mentioned in chapter 1. The first is the 120 of Acts 1:15 and this group is "probably" the one commonly assumed by the commentaries to be the subject pronoun of Acts 2:1, and therefore the initial recipients of the gift of the Holy Spirit on the Day of Pentecost. However, this interpretation fails in one simple grammatical test: it is not the closest antecedent* to Acts 2:1.

*Antecedent is the grammatical term used to refer to the noun that a pronoun replaces. An antecedent comes before a pronoun. A pronoun and its antecedent must agree in gender and number. For example, if the antecedent is singular and female, the pronoun must refer to a single female.

Since we know that the chapter divisions are not part of any manuscript copy of the book and first appeared in the Wycliffe English Bible of 1382, we can safely ignore them and read Acts 1:26 (the last verse of that chapter) and then Acts 2:1. *"[26]And they cast lots for them, and the lot fell on Matthias, and he was numbered with the eleven apostles. [1][And] when the day of Pentecost arrived, they were all together in one place."* Remember the math: eleven plus one equals twelve, not 120. The 120 are clearly stated in Acts 1:15 and referred to by the pronoun "they" in verses 23, 24, and finally at the start of verse 26. Then Luke talks about Matthias being *"numbered with the eleven apostles,"* or *"he was added to and counted with the eleven apostles"* (AMP) and the new Twelve become the nearest antecedent group to Acts 2:1.

Lest you think this is some new idea I made up, I searched to find commentaries that handle it in the way I describe. The latest study Bible I have on my shelf was published in 2008 (ESV) and the translation committee chose to comment on the word "all" and ignore the "they." Their footnote reads, *"All* most likely includes the entire 120 assembled in the upper room (1:15)," in order to conform to the accepted traditional teaching of this event.

In John McGarvey's *Commentary on Acts* (1872), he discusses the same "antecedent confusion" that I just pointed out to you, and then writes: "The apostles alone, therefore, are said to have been filled with the Holy Spirit. This conclusion is not only evident from the context, but it is required by the very terms of the promise concerning the Holy Spirit. It was to the apostles alone, on the night of the betrayal, that Jesus had promised the miraculous aid of the Spirit, and to them alone he had said, on the day of ascension, 'You shall be immersed in the Holy Spirit.' It involves both a perversion of the text, and a misconception of the design of the event... to suppose that the immersion in the Holy Spirit was shared by the whole hundred and twenty." [You can download his commentary at http:// *icotb.org/resources/Acts-McGarvey-Original.pdf*.]

Coffman's *Acts (Coffman New Testament Commentaries, Vol. 5, 1974)* takes a similar viewpoint: "'They were all together'... Who were the 'they'? Scholars disagree radically about this; but the conviction here is that the reference is to the Twelve. They were the only ones to whom Jesus had promised such an outpouring of the Spirit. Furthermore, Peter's words (Acts 2:32) that 'we are all witnesses' of Christ's resurrection can refer only to the Twelve, because only two disciples were found among the whole one hundred and twenty who were eligible to join them as 'witnesses.'

"What the word 'all' surely means in Acts 2:32 must therefore be the meaning here [Acts 2:1]. 'We... all,' as used by Peter, identifies the 'they... all,' as used here by Luke. Also, *'numbered with the eleven apostles,'* as it stands at the end of Acts 1, requires 'eleven apostles' to be understood as the antecedent of 'they' in Acts 2:1. DeWelt said: 'The fact that the antecedent of any pronoun is found by referring back to the nearest noun (or pronoun) with which it agrees in number, etc., clinches the argument of the baptism of only the apostles in the Holy Spirit.'"

Finally, Mark Dunagan's *Commentary on the Bible* adds these points: "The only men speaking by inspiration upon this day will be the 12 apostles (2:14)... The crowd addressed their question to the apostles—inferring [implying], they were the only ones manifesting that the Spirit had come upon them (2:37)." So, eleven plus one still equals twelve, and this applies to Acts chapter 2 verses 2, 3, 4 and 14 as well. Only the Twelve who were sitting in the "house" (verse 2) had the tongues of fire sitting on them (verse 3). The "place" of verse 1, the "house" of verse 2 was very likely [Olshausen] "one of the thirty spacious rooms around the temple court, described by Josephus and called *oikoi,* houses, is most agreeable to all the facts" (McGarvey).

The Greek word is used of a dwelling but also as a building, such as the Tabernacle and the Temple. We do the same in English. We speak of our Opera House which is really a theater, or a full house when a concert is sold out in an entertainment center.

Jesus quoted an incident involving David in Matthew 12:4, *"How he entered the house of God and ate the bread of the Presence..."* Other examples use the term "the house of God" (Matthew 12:4, Mark 2:26, John 2:16). So the usage of the word "house" requires the context to understand its meaning. Since the context speaks of it happening at a prayer hour and a "multitude" hearing, seeing and questioning the signs and wonders (Acts 2:6), it fits the Temple though it is not as strong an indication as the grammatical proof.

Only the Twelve spoke in tongues (verse 4), even though there was a "multitude" present (verse 6). In addition, the recipients were Galileans (Acts 2:7), whereas the 120 in Jerusalem more than likely were predominantly Judeans.

"[And] when the day of Pentecost arrived, **they** *[the Twelve] were all together in one place"* (Acts 2:1). The Holy

Spirit descended on the them at the third hour (Jewish time), 9 a.m. Roman time, which was an hour of prayer (verse 15). This is indicated by the "multitude" present who could not have squeezed into an upper room, but did hear *"the sound like a rushing wind,"* *(Acts 2:2)* followed by the speaking in tongues, *"we hear them telling in our own tongues the mighty works of God"* (Acts 2:11), coming from one of the rooms around the temple court.

We are told in verse 15 that this event occurred at "the third hour of the day," which was the first hour of prayer. The apostles were still maintaining the Jewish way of life (Acts 2:46; 3:1) and at the third hour, 9 a.m., they would have been in the temple praying, not at the place where they were staying in Jerusalem.

I'm amazed at the preachers who declare that this event took place in the Upper Room. These same preachers expect their members and office holders to be at the Wednesday night prayer meetings (if they still have them), but declare that the apostles skipped this hour of prayer because they were still in the Upper Room where they were staying (Acts 1:13). There is no logic in that stance.

To complete the record, in verse 3 *"And divided tongues as of fire appeared to them and rested on each one of them."* McGarvey writes: "We see, then, flaming tongues, like flames of fire, distributed so that one rests upon each of the Twelve apostles. In the clause, 'it sat upon each of them,' the singular pronoun it is used after the plural tongues, to indicate that not all, but only one of the tongues sat upon each apostle, the term distributed having already suggested the contemplation of them singly."

I can imagine the Twelve hearing the sound effect of

wind blowing and seeing the tongue of fire on each other's heads. Just as they were about to lift their hands in worship (well, they were the original Pentecostals!) and say, "Wow! Thank you, Jesus," instead they heard themselves speaking strange words!

"And they were all filled [God did the filling] *with the Holy Spirit* [the gift] *and began to speak* [they did the speaking using the same mechanics as usual] *in other tongues as the Spirit* [the giver] *gave them utterance [words to utter]"* (Acts 2:4). "We see this [the flaming tongues of fire], and we hear all the Twelve at once speaking in languages to them unknown. We see a divine power present with these men, for to no other power can we attribute those tongues. We hear the unmistakable effects of a divine power acting upon their minds; for no other power could give them an instantaneous knowledge of languages which they had never studied" (McGarvey).

Finis Dake in his *Annotated Reference Bible* wrote: "This was similar to the Spirit speaking through the prophets in their own language (Acts 3:21; Hebrews 1:1-2), only here it was with different languages (v.4,6,11)."

The word "other" is *heteros,* a Greek word indicating other of a different kind, while Greek also has *allos,* meaning other of the same kind. "Tongues" means by implication, languages, as translated by AMP, CEV, CSB, NET, etc.

"⁵Now there were dwelling in Jerusalem Jews, devout men from every nation under heaven. ⁶and at this sound the multitude came together, and they were bewildered, because each one was hearing them speak in his own language. ⁷And they were amazed and astonished, saying, 'Are not all these who are speaking Galileans? ⁸And how is it that

we hear, each of us in his own native language? ⁹Parthians and Medes and Elamites and residents of Mesopotamia, Judea and Cappadocia, Pontus and Asia, ¹⁰Phrygia and Pamphylia, Egypt and the parts of Libya belonging to Cyrene, and visitors from Rome, ¹¹both Jews and proselytes, Cretans and Arabians—we hear them telling in our own tongues the mighty works of God.'"

The honest reader is left with no doubt of the veracity of verse 4, when the Twelve *"began to speak in other tongues as the Spirit gave them utterance."* There is no indication of how long they spoke in the unlearned languages. However, given the questions that were being spoken out aloud around them and the mocking of others (verse 13) with accusations of drunkenness, *"Peter, standing with the eleven"* (verse 14) took the lead and started speaking in the common language of *"the men of Israel"* (verse 22), and everybody quieted down to hear his words, both the tongue speakers and the *"devout men from every nation under heaven."*

In summary then, the promise of the gift of the Holy Spirit was given to the Twelve apostles by Jesus; the antecedent of the subject pronoun "they" in Acts 2:1 is the eleven plus one in Acts 1:26; and the crowd addressed their questions (Acts 2:8,12) to the apostles—implying they were the only ones who were speaking in tongues at that time.

So there we have the participants and the place for this momentous day, the coming of the Spirit, and what was to be known as the birthday of the church.

6

The Purpose of Pentecost

It may come as surprise to some Pentecostal, Charismatic and Word of Faith believers that the main purpose of the Day of Pentecost was not to make speaking in tongues available to believers. The experience was certainly part of the package, as is clearly seen in Acts chapter 2, but when Jesus taught his disciples about what was about to happen, only once did he mention speaking in a "new tongues" and that was on the day of his Ascension.

"And these signs will accompany those who believe: in my name they will cast out demons; they will speak in new tongues" (Mark 16:17). No mention there of seeking to speak in tongues; just that this experience "will accompany those who believe." The KJV says "will follow" and for some Christians the experience is following so far behind them that you can't see it!

I speak in tongues, as do millions of Christians, and I encourage others to enjoy the blessing. But this experience is not the "be-all and end-all" of the Christian life. Perhaps the words of Paul in I Corinthians 13:1 should be quoted in this context: *"If I speak with human eloquence and angelic ecstasy but don't love, I'm nothing but the creaking of a rusty gate"* (MSG). Also on display that first day was the power to witness effectively (promised in Acts 1:8), when 3,000 people were added to the church. Then there was later displayed the power to heal, to perform signs and wonders, to demonstrate the boldness of the disciples of Jesus.

Let's look again at what Jesus said about the coming Day of Pentecost and see if he reveals its purpose. *"For John baptized with water, but you will be baptized with the Holy Spirit not many days from now"* (Acts 1:5). The word "baptized" means to be covered wholly with a fluid, to be totally immersed in the subject, here for John it is water, and for the current believers it is spirit, "not many days from now." In Luke's gospel he writes of soon being *"clothed with power from on high"* (Luke 24:49), completely covered with power, wall-to-wall power. The power was dynamic (from the Greek word *dunamis*, here translated as "power"). This is therefore more comprehensive than in the Old Testament when the spirit came upon certain individuals for a period of time for a particular task. In John's gospel we learn that *"the Spirit of truth... dwells with you and will be in you,"* that is, within the believer when the Comforter has come (John 14:17).

"Whoever believes in me will also do the works that I do; and greater works than these will he do, because I am going to the Father" (John 14:12). It is difficult to believe this means greater in quality but certainly can mean greater in quantity. Instead of just a few people, thousands times thousands would be doing the same works as Jesus did.

Acts 10:38 is a summary of the ministry of Jesus: *"God anointed Jesus of Nazareth with the Holy Spirit and with power. He went about doing good and healing all who were oppressed by the devil, for God was with him. "* And on the day of Pentecost, God anointed the believers with the same spirit and power (Luke 24:49) so they could go about doing good and healing the sick, for they would know God is with them.

"And I will ask the Father, and he will give you another Helper, to be with you forever, even the Spirit of truth…" (John 14:16-17). "Another" here means another of the same kind, not different but similar. KJV uses the word "Comforter" and the Amplified Bible adds "Counselor, Helper, Intercessor, Advocate, Strengthener, and Standby." Can you say "Amen" to that? Whatever Jesus was to his disciples, the spirit is to us. *"But the Helper, the Holy Spirit, whom the Father will send in my name, he will teach you all things and bring to your remembrance all that I have said to you"* (John 14:26). So we can add Teacher to the list.

"But when the Helper comes, whom I will send to you from the Father, the Spirit of truth, who proceeds from the Father, he will bear witness about me" (John 15:26). So, the spirit within will help us to know Jesus more intimately—his attitudes, will, desires for our lives. The spirit helps us to be what Annie Johnson Flint described in her poem: "Christ has no hands but our hands to do His work today."

"When the Spirit of truth comes, he will guide you into all the truth, for he will not speak on his own authority, but whatever he hears he will speak, and he will declare to you the things that are to come. [14]He will glorify me, for he will take what is mine and declare it to you. All

that the Father has is mine; therefore I said that he will take what is mine and declare it to you" (John 16:13-14). The spirit is again our teacher, guiding us into all truth. In internet terms, the spirit provides the answers to our questions like an FAQ page or Google search does. The spirit is like a GPS device, showing us the road to follow.

"But you will receive power when [not after] *the Holy Spirit has come upon you, and you will be my witnesses in Jerusalem and in all Judea and Samaria, and to the end of the earth"* (Acts 1:8). The believers started to fulfill this statement on the Day of Pentecost, when the multitude of Jews from other nations heard *"them telling in our own tongues the mighty works of God"* (Acts 2:11b). The Lord added 3,000 believers to the family of God in Acts chapter 2 and another 5,000 (or increased to 5,000) in Acts chapter 4, and millions since.

7

The Doubters of Pentecost

"But others mocking said, 'They are filled with new wine'" (Acts 2:13)—yes, there were doubters on the Day of Pentecost. *"Do not forbid speaking in tongues"* Paul commanded around 20 years later, but ignored now by many church leaders. *"We have not even heard that there is a Holy Spirit"* (Acts 19:2)—around the same time there were Christians were still ignorant of the events of the Day of Pentecost. And we still have doubters and ignorant Christians today.

Before leaving Acts 2:4 and the speaking in languages not learned, I need to emphasize that the glossolalia (the academic term) is always languages, not "gibberish" as critics of the experience often claim in this century. There are many incidents reported in books and magazines of other people recognizing the words that are being spoken by a believer who has no idea of what they are saying.

Just because the critic, as a hearer, does not know the language is not proof that it is "gibberish" or "hocus pocus." Linguists estimate that there are currently around 7,097 languages being used in the world today (2019, *https://www.ethnologue.com/*). Those critics are going to find it impossible to locate a person who knows all the languages in order to make a judgment. Linguists estimate something like 31,000 languages have existed in human history (*https://www.quora.com/How-many-human-languages-have-ever-existed-on-Earth*). I have just read that there are 200 languages in use in the state in which I reside, and I doubt if there is one person who is familiar with all 200.

Another type of critic is a *cessationist,* as opposed to a *continuationist.* One of the cessationist's beliefs is that the gifts (or manifestations, I Corinthians 12:7), including speaking in tongues, were terminated near the end of the apostolic age and are no longer required now, so we are seeing satanic imitations. Check out the article on "Cessationists" on Wikipedia, or read Dr. Jon Ruthvens book *On the Cessation of the Charismata (1993, 2008),* a detailed academic essay against the view of the cessationists.

Long after New Testament times, Iraneus (130-202 A.D.), a Greek bishop and eventually martyr, wrote in his book V and VI, "In like manner we do also hear many brethren in the church, who possess prophetic gifts, and who through the Spirit speak all kinds of languages, and bring to light for the general benefit the hidden things of men, and declare the mysteries of God." Justin, Tertullian, Origen, and even Augustine (354-430) wrote that the gifts of the Spirit were still present in the church. And down through the Church Age records indicate that there was no cessation of these spiritual manifestations or gifts.

The 1906 Azusa Street outpouring in Los Angeles was not "another Pentecost" but a special "sign and wonder" to the universal church. It was birthed in much prayer and included speaking and also singing in tongues to an unknown melody, a heavy mist or fog that permeated the meeting room, flames of fire seen above the building with the fire department called out several times. In the meetings, prayer was the emphasis and divine healings were simultaneously happening as believers prayed one for another, and later a sermon was given by William Seymour (see Frank Bartleman's account, *The Azusa Street Revival— An Eyewitness Account,* Whitaker, 2008).

On the Acts 2 Day of Pentecost, the outpouring was not birthed in prayer, the disciples being told to simply wait in the city of Jerusalem. They went to the temple at the hours of prayer as was their custom. There was not a 10-day prayer meeting. When the day *"was fully come,"* they heard the noise of wind and saw the tongue of fire over the heads of each of the 12 apostles, who then spoke in tongues in various recognized languages listed in Acts 2:9-11a: *"⁹Parthians and Medes and Elamites and residents of Mesopotamia, Judea and Cappadocia, Pontus and Asia, ¹⁰Phrygia and Pamphylia, Egypt and the parts of Libya belonging to Cyrene, and visitors from Rome, ¹¹both Jews and proselytes, Cretans and Arabians."*

"Beginning with the farthest east, the Parthians, the enumeration proceeds farther and farther westward till it comes to Judea; next come the western countries, from Cappadocia to Pamphylia; then the southern, from Egypt to Cyrene; finally, apart from all geographical consideration, Cretes and Arabians are placed together. This enumeration is evidently designed to convey an impression of universality" [Baumgarten, quoted in Jamieson, Fausset, Brown].

Then the tongues ceased as people asked the apostles questions and Peter replied and gave a recounting of the death and resurrection of Christ and made "an altar call," as evangelicals would call it (see verses 12-40).

In my lifetime we have had the charismatic renewal among mainline denominational churches, and now it is common to have believers who speak in tongues, and there is no sign of it ceasing. Over 100 million Christians are recognized today as being Pentecostal.

So what is different about the first Pentecostal outpouring and what we see today? In the Dake's *Annotated Reference Bible,* there are these comments on Acts 2: "Though speaking in tongues is done through immediate inspiration by new recipients when one has thus received the gift, it then becomes a part of his [or her] mental make-up so that he can, if he desires to do so, exercise it without direct inspiration," such as in I Corinthians 13:1-3 to which he refers. He goes on to say, "This is why the exercise of vocal gifts of prophecy, tongues, and interpretation of tongues is commanded to be regulated and even judged as to whether it be under direction inspiration or whether a person is exercising a gift of himself" (I Corinthians 14:29-33)."

Verse 32 of that passage states, *"and the spirits of prophets are subject to prophets,"* and since I Corinthians chapters 12 and 14 show the similarities between the three vocal manifestations of speaking in tongues, interpretation of tongues, and prophecy, he applies verse 32 to speaking in tongues also (as do many Pentecostals).

Smith Wigglesworth (1859-1947), a highly respected British independent evangelist and known as the Apostle of Faith, visited the United States several times and on one occasion preached in a large Assemblies of God camp meeting in California. In the audience was J.E. Stiles, an Assemblies of God preacher. As George Stormont wrote in his book *Wigglesworth: A Man Who Walked with God* (Tulsa: Harrison House, 1989, pp.52-54), Wigglesworth was concerned about those who had received the gift of the Spirit with speaking in tongues but had not spoken in tongues in the last six months. He asked those who fit into that category to stand, and instructed them on "the first step of faith." When he said "Go" they were to speak in tongues and then he would shout "Stop." J.E. Stiles did not believe this would happen, but to his amazement that is exactly what happened and he was speaking in tongues too! Then Wigglesworth cried out, "Hold it!" and the meeting became quiet.

Learning that the Holy Spirit operates on faith so affected J.E. Stiles that he gave up having tarrying meetings, and wrote the best-selling volume *The Gift of the Holy Spirit*. In my city a Pentecostal preacher with the largest congregation banned them from reading the book, which would have helped sales no end! It is now widely accepted that believers can exercise the speaking in tongues by an exercise of their will.

I learned an essential lesson as a young Christian, and that was not to take my theology from hymns or praise and worship songs, but only from the Bible. For example, in the denomination in which I was brought up, we sang this song written by William Booth, the founder:

> Thou Christ of burning, cleansing flame,
> Send the fire, send the fire, send the fire!
> Thy blood-bought gift today we claim,
> Send the fire, send the fire, send the fire!
> Look down and see this waiting host,
> Give us the promised Holy Ghost;
> We want another Pentecost,
> Send the fire, send the fire, send the fire!

I'm not convinced that "We want another Pentecost."
Why do we need it when we can use the fire that God
supplied centuries ago? "Give us the promised Holy Ghost?"
Didn't Peter call it "the *gift* of the Holy Spirit"? When a
gift is given to you, what do you do? Ask for it to be
given again? No, you receive it. Giving and receiving go
together. Yet receiving requires an action; you take it out
of the hand of the one giving it. Many of God's promises
are voice-activated, so thank Him for it and use the gift
for His glory.

The church in which I met my wife had the same doctrinal
background as mine, but their *Church Manual* made it
clear that the Christian experience was performance based,
requiring their members to not go to theaters, circuses,
movies, and like places of public entertainment, not to
engage in public bathing, not to drink alcohol or smoke
or chew tobacco, not to read the newspaper on Sunday,
and so the list went on. In 1972 their General Assembly
moved that "Any practice and/or propagation of speaking
in tongues, either as the evidence of the baptism with the
Holy Spirit or neo-Pentecostal ecstatic prayer language
shall be interpreted as inveighing against the doctrines
and usages of the church..." and encouraged those believing
these doctrines to find another church, which they did.
So even though these evident truths are believed and practiced
across many denominations and individual churches, it
seems certain that there will always be differences of opinion
in the Christian life.

In summary, on the weight of the evidence in the Word,
there is neither a restatement of the command to wait,
nor is there a repetition of the signs seen on the Day of

Pentecost. Therefore to sing about "another Pentecost" is an inaccurate representation of the Word of God. The book of Acts does record other incidents where people spoke in tongues when they received "the gift of the Holy Spirit" (the term always used after the Day of Pentecost), but without the "signs and wonders" of sounds of wind and seeing cloven tongues of fire. When we discover who we are in Christ and that we have Christ in us, we should realize that we have wall-to-wall Holy Spirit within us also and can be a real witness for Christ to a dying world.

Now we can sing,

> I'm rejoicing night and day As I walk the pilgrim way,
> For the hand of God in all my life I see,
> And the reason of my bliss Yes, the secret all is this,
> That the Comforter abides with me.
> *(Herbert Buffum).*

Now its becomes personal: "the Comforter abides with me." In John 14:16 Jesus said the Comforter would *"be with you forever"* and in verse 17 he says *"for he dwells with you and will be in you"* [referring to the coming Day of Pentecost].

There are more Bible verses I haven't quoted, but you have enough to see the magnificence of God's plan in sending the spirit on the Day of Pentecost to all believers. Let us rejoice together on the Day of Pentecost for this gift from our loving Father.

8

The First Christian Sermon

The life of Peter is an interesting study, and because my parents saw fit to give me his name, I have been known to defend him. Prior to this moment, he had some great ups and some deep downs. The incident I like best is when he walked on the water toward Jesus, recorded in Matthew 14:22-33 and also in Mark and John. I have written of this elsewhere. Everyone remembers his worst moment, when he denied Christ on the night before His death in Matthew 26:69-75.

However, the death, resurrection, and ascension of Christ must have had a huge effect on Peter. When the Jews were crying out for an explanation of what was happening as the Apostles spoke in tongues, Peter didn't miss a beat and began to preach. *"12And all were amazed and perplexed, saying to one another, 'What does this mean?' 13But others mocking said, 'They are filled with new wine.' 14But Peter, standing with the eleven, lifted up his voice and addressed them."* God bless Peter, and how we need less of the seeker-friendly style of preaching and more of Peter's direct style as given here in Acts!

"14bMen of Judea and all who dwell in Jerusalem, let this be known to you, and give ear to my words. 15For

these people are not drunk, as you suppose, since it is only the third hour of the day." What a great introduction! Every preacher has to know the audience to which they are preaching. On this occasion in the temple, they were "church people," believed in God, obeyed His worship commandments, and were well-versed in the Old Testament scriptures.

So Peter started quoting from the prophet Joel: *"But this is what was uttered through the prophet Joel:*[17]*'And in the last days it shall be, God declares, that I will pour out my Spirit on all flesh, and your sons and your daughters shall prophesy, and your young men shall see visions, and your old men shall dream dreams;* [18]*even on my male servants and female servants in those days I will pour out my Spirit, and they shall prophesy.* [19]*And I will show wonders in the heavens above and signs on the earth below, blood, and fire, and vapor of smoke;* [20]*the sun shall be turned to darkness and the moon to blood, before the day of the Lord comes, the great and magnificent day.* [21]*And it shall come to pass that everyone who calls upon the name of the Lord shall be saved'"* (Acts 2:16-21). Peter was quoting from memory Joel 2:28-32a as his text, and in doing so gave evidence that the Day of Pentecost was the fulfillment of the prophecy given to Israel in c.795 BC.

Next he spoke with great clarity and directness to these religious people. *"*[22]*Men of Israel, hear these words: Jesus of Nazareth, a man attested to you by God with mighty works and wonders and signs that God did through him in your midst, as you yourselves know—*[23]*this Jesus, delivered up according to the definite plan and foreknowledge of God, you crucified and killed by the hands of lawless men.*

24God raised him up, loosing the pangs of death, because it was not possible for him to be held by it." Now that got their attention! We learn later in chapter 4 that there were probably temple guards watching and listening on the edge of the crowd. They would have reported the events to their captain and he would have told the High Priest. It was not the accusation of "you crucified and killed" that concerned the authorities, it was the "God raised him up" declaration of the resurrection of Jesus from the dead.

Then Peter quoted from David, as recorded in Psalm 16:8-11. *"25For David says concerning him* [the Messiah], *'I saw the Lord always before me, for he is at my right hand that I may not be shaken; 26therefore my heart was glad, and my tongue rejoiced; my flesh also will dwell in hope. 27For you will not abandon my soul to Hades, or let your Holy One see corruption. 28You have made known to me the paths of life; you will make me full of gladness with your presence'"* (Acts 2:25-28).

Next, Peter applied the Old Testament scripture to the current event, as he did with Joel, but this time he used the "patriarch David." *"29Brothers, I may say to you with confidence about the patriarch David that he both died and was buried, and his tomb is with us to this day. 30Being therefore a prophet, and knowing that God had sworn with an oath to him that he would set one of his descendants on his throne, 31he foresaw and spoke about the resurrection of the Christ, that he was not abandoned to Hades, nor did his flesh see corruption. 32This Jesus God raised up, and of that we all are witnesses. 33Being therefore exalted at the right hand of God, and having received from the Father the promise of the Holy Spirit, he has poured out this that you yourselves are seeing and hearing.* ³⁴*For David did not ascend into the heavens, but he himself says, 'The Lord said to my Lord, Sit at my right hand,* ³⁵*until I make your enemies your footstool.'* ³⁶*Let all the house of Israel therefore know for certain that God has made him both Lord and Christ, this Jesus whom you crucified"* (Acts 2:29-36).

The crowd was now under great conviction and didn't wait for Peter's call to action, but cried out. *"Now when they heard this they were cut to the heart, and said to Peter and the rest of the apostles, 'Brothers, what shall we do?'"* (Acts 2:37). Any preacher would give his right arm for a response like that to a sermon! So, Peter gave them his answer: *"*³⁸*And Peter said to them, 'Repent and be baptized every one of you in the name of Jesus Christ for the forgiveness of your sins, and you will receive the gift of the Holy Spirit.* ³⁹*For the promise is for you and for your children and for all who are far off, everyone whom the Lord our God calls to himself.'* ⁴⁰*And with many other words he bore witness and continued to exhort them, saying, 'Save yourselves from this crooked generation'"* (Acts 2:38-40). The response was immediate: *"So those who received his word were baptized, and there were added that day about three thousand souls"* (Acts 2:41)! In McGarvey's Commentary on Acts, he demonstrates how it was indeed possible to baptize 3,000 people in water in one day in Jerusalem. (See page 30 to download your copy of his commentary.)

9

The Daily Life of a Believer

Let us look at a summary statement of perhaps the first few weeks after Pentecost in Acts 2:42-47. Summaries are a unique feature of Acts, such as the common religious life of early believers in Acts 2:42-47; the sharing of goods among believers in Acts 4:32-35; miracles performed by the apostles in Acts 5:12-16; Paul's ministry for two years at Ephesus in Acts 19:10; and the ministry of Jesus in Acts 10:37-39. Since the book covers approximately 33 years, it is a valid method of narrative to give such generalizations and to only select individual incidents out of many. The final verse of John's gospel aptly describes the value of summaries: *"Now there are also many other things that Jesus did. Were every one of them to be written, I suppose that the world itself could not contain the books that would be written"* (John 21:25).

"And they devoted themselves to the apostles' teaching and the fellowship, [and] to the breaking of bread and the prayers" (ESV). You can read the whole section down the end of the chapter, verse 47. The many repetitions of the word "and" (KJV) in verse 42 encourage us to slowly work through each statement to understand its full impact.

Learners

"They devoted themselves to the apostles' teaching...;"
"they continued steadfastly..." (KJV). There's the secret
of the early church. It was not a system of daily devotions
but people devoted daily to the apostles' teaching from
the Word of God. They were hungry to hear the "proven
truth, not peripheral truth." They were after the apostles'
teaching, not the teaching from the self-proclaimed super-
spiritual person or the "young in the faith" believer who
has just discovered a fascinating verse. And they not only
wanted to learn what the Lord had said, but they wanted
to do the signs and wonders that the Lord had done.

Just a few weeks earlier the twelve apostles had heard
the Great Commission from the lips of Jesus. *"Go therefore
and make disciples [learners] of all nations ..."* (Matthew
28:19). He didn't say get decisions for Christ or have them
repeat a prayer after you. Jesus said that the twelve should
"make learners," people who were hungry to learn. "Make
them, mark them, mature them" (verses 19-20).

So Peter taught the gospel on the Day of Pentecost
and the crowd responded with *"Brothers, what shall we
do?"*(Acts 2:37) And the first thing he told them was to
*"repent and be baptized every one of you in the name of
Jesus Christ for the forgiveness of your sins, and you will
receive the gift of the Holy Spirit"* (verse38). The teaching
was about Jesus, and after "many other words" they were
added to the worldwide church. I know one Charismatic
offshoot that was strong on "biblical accuracy" yet taught
how wonderful it was that you could speak in tongues
without having to go through repentance. That's not what
Peter taught here.

Paul's revelation of our total union with Christ by grace came later, but at this point the Apostles had not connected the dots in Jesus' teaching that preceded the fullness of truth to come.

The "sound doctrine [teaching]" of I Timothy 1:10 and the "pattern of sound words" of II Timothy 1:13 was music to the ears of the earnest believers of the early church, and the same is true of hungry hearts today. Just around the corner were difficult times, *"For the time is coming when people will not endure sound teaching, but having itching ears they will accumulate for themselves teachers to suit their own passions, and will turn away from listening to the truth and wander off into myths"* (II Timothy 4:3-4) And those days are well and truly established now in the 21st century church.

Fellowship

Acts 2:42 is a summary statement of the first few weeks of the impact of Pentecost. *"And they continued steadfastly in the apostles' doctrine and fellowship..."* (KJV). Not only did the new believers devote themselves to the teaching the apostles gave, but they also felt a desire for fellowship.

A definition of fellowship that I heard decades ago is "two fellows in one ship." In this verse it is fellowship "in its largest sense" (Jamieson, Fausset and Brown commentary), and the Greek word means a sharer in a common interest. It is not a reference to an organized local Christian fellowship, which did not exist at this time, but rather to believers everywhere. The ESV is the only major translation that renders the word as an entity, "the fellowship," so I accept the majority opinion that it refers to a commonality. "They were like family to each other" (CEV). Paul later taught that the Church wherever it is located is one great family of God. When you become a believer you have two families: a biological one and a spiritual one. The spiritual family can often be more attractive.

There is much talk and emphasis on Kingdom teaching and position these days, and the Kingdom of God certainly gets mentioned in Acts and the Pauline epistles. Yet the primary illustration of the relationship between God and the believer is that of a family. He is our Father, we are His sons and daughters and heirs, and we have siblings.

I lived in England for 10 years, from age 5 to 15, and it was a good life to be a subject of a benevolent king. But it is even better to be a prince or princess with almost unlimited access and privileges! So I boldly proclaim that I'm a son of God with power and authority. The blue blood of the King of Kings runs in my spiritual veins. I've got status in the family and a life-long relationship.

Why do we need other Christians? How about encouragement, edifying (building up), enthusiasm (God-in-us-ism)? *"What then, brothers? When you come together, each one has a hymn, a lesson, a revelation, a tongue, or an interpretation. Let all things be done for building up"* (I Corinthians 14:26). While I believe that you could exist on a small desert island with just Christ in you, I cannot ignore the many later references in Acts and the Epistles to the helpfulness of other believers.

We are slipping into a cocooning world and rubbing shoulders less often with other people. Many no longer know their neighbor's names, let alone have a friendship with them. In this Internet world, we may have hundreds of "likes" on a Facebook page, yet there is still something missing, and that is the give and take of one-on-one friendships with like-minded people.

So take advantage of the common interest you have with other believers, *"for you are all one in Christ Jesus"* (Galatians 3:28). Jesus said to the Father, *"The glory that you have given me I have given to them, that they may be one even as we are one, I in them and you in me, that they may become perfectly one..."* (John 17:22-23a).

Breaking of bread

I now move on to the third item in the summary, the breaking of bread. *"And they devoted themselves to the apostles' teaching and* [omit "the"] *fellowship, to the breaking of bread..."* (Acts 2:42). The translation of the term "breaking of bread" in the KJV is correct. One paraphrase version, however, attempts to be helpful by translating it as "sharing in the Lord's Supper" (NLT), but the phrase is not limited to that. The Amplified Bible translates it, "to the breaking of bread [including the Lord's Supper]," footnoting "many authorities." So it could refer to both a common meal and the Lord's Supper, or Holy Communion or the Eucharist, depending on which tradition you come from. Often it depends on the context as to which meal is in sight, and in many commentaries we read that it may have been normal to have a common meal first with fellow believers and then observe the Lord's Supper.

In many ways this third aspect of "continuing steadfastly" follows on from fellowship, as eating a meal together is a deeper expression of fellowship. In Eastern countries you had an obligation to be kind to strangers and to give them a meal before sending them on the rest of their journey. However, the master of the house would never sit down and eat with a stranger, though he would with his relatives and friends.

This custom gives new light to the Lord's statement in Revelation 3:20, *"Behold, I stand at the door and knock. If anyone hears my voice and opens the door, I will come in to him and eat with him, and he with me"* (ESV). Here the divine guest becomes the host, as He is the Lord of all, and He becomes a friend or better still a relative.

In Acts 2:46 the same term is used of the common meal: *"breaking bread in their homes, they received their food with glad and generous hearts."* In Acts 20:7, many years later, *"On the first day of the week, when we were gathered together to break bread,"* in other words, to partake of the Lord's Supper. *"And he took bread, and when he had given thanks, he broke it and gave it to them, saying, This is my body, which is given for you.* **Do this in** *remembrance of me"* (Luke 22:19).

As a child I was brought up in a tradition that never obeyed this command of the Lord, because it was felt that drinking wine was too great a temptation for recovered or recovering drunkards. (Don't let the Word get in the way of what you do!) When I started attending other denominations around 20+ years old, I observed that there was a special reverence by Christians in this part of the service. Later when training for the ministry, we were taught that the broken body of Jesus was for our physical healing and the shed blood was for our spiritual healing, and I still view it that way today. I like receiving the bread and thanking God for my health and healing, and receiving the wine or grape juice and thanking God for my salvation and sonship privileges.

Some of the evangelical churches I've been involved with or visited have communion every Sunday, others once a month, and the most scriptural: *"For **as often** as you eat this bread and drink the cup, you proclaim the Lord's death until he comes"* (I Corinthians 11:26). "As often" means exactly what it says, "every time" (AMP, MSG, NET, NLT). So no legalistic rule is laid down for the church, apart from "every time" you do so remember his death and his second coming. It is "the link between His two comings, the monument of the one, the pledge of the other..." (Frédéric Godet).

Prayers

"And they continued steadfastly in the apostles' doctrine and fellowship, in the breaking of bread, and in prayers" (KJV). I now move on to the fourth item, prayers. This can be understood in two ways, as some translations use the term "and the prayers," that is, ritualistic or commonly repeated prayers, such as in the temple (Acts 3:1) and prayers "from the heart" in their homes, such as when the opposition was so strong they felt a need for God to do something special (Acts 4:23).

First, we can take it as it reads in the KJV. There is no question that the original twelve disciples knew what it meant to pray. Take, for example, the passage where they asked Jesus, *"Lord, teach us to pray"* (Luke 11:1). He immediately answered, *"When you pray, say..."* and gave them what the Church calls the Lord's Prayer but is better called the Disciples' Prayer.

In the same chapter Luke records the promise of prayer, *"⁹And I tell you, ask, and it will be given to you; seek, and you will find; knock, and it will be opened to you. ¹⁰For everyone who asks receives, and the one who seeks finds, and to the one who knocks it will be opened"* (verse 9,10). What comfort this triple assurance of answered prayer gives us! On numerous occasions, Jesus plainly said to his disciples, "Pray!" He himself spent time alone with God in prayer, so the example and exhortation to pray was constantly present.

Jesus also taught how not to pray. In Matthew's account of the Luke 11 incident we read, *"⁵And when you pray, you must not be like the hypocrites. For they love to stand and pray in the synagogues and at the street corners, that they may be seen by others. Truly, I say to you, they have received their reward... ⁷And when you pray, do not heap up empty phrases as the Gentiles do, for they think that they will be heard for their many words"* (Matthew 6:5,7).

I am reminded of D.L. Moody who had asked a man in a service to pray a closing prayer, and he prayed around the world a couple of times! While he was still praying, Moody got to his feet and said, "While our brother is finishing his prayer we'll sing the closing hymn!" I've heard plenty of those kinds of prayer.

So, the disciples were taught to pray. Whether they grasped the importance of it or not we don't know. (Jesus did say they were slow on the uptake!) Also remember that Acts 2:42 is not just about the 11 remaining original disciples but also the 3,000 who were added to the church (Acts 2:41) after Peter's sermon on the Day of Pentecost. Apart from that sermon in these early chapters of the Acts, we don't have much record of what was included in "the apostles' teaching" (verse 42). Yet some kind of praying was observed.

The issue is further complicated when we remember that this was truly a Jewish Pentecost and the participants were of the Jewish faith (Acts 2:5). Even the apostles were still keeping the Jewish traditions, as was evident by Peter and John going up to the temple at the hour of prayer (Acts 3:1).

The modern example of this period might be the charismatic movement in the mainline denominations in the late 1950s. These Christians discovered a far greater depth of experience in their knowledge of the Holy Spirit and spoke in other languages as in Acts 2:4, yet initially they still went to their denominational churches and were comfortable with their ritual. Later many were given the "left foot of fellowship" and sent on their way when they persisted in the experience.

Translations with the definite article "the prayers" (which is in the Greek text) include the ASV, ESV, and GNB. Wuest renders it, "to the gatherings where prayers to God were offered," which is a good explanatory paraphrase. So, it is just as likely in context that the "prayers" were communal prayers that had been repeated for centuries in the Jewish religion, or even the Disciples' Prayer that Jesus had taught the Twelve.

All this says that prayer is important. *"Continue steadfastly in prayer, being watchful in it with thanksgiving"* (Colossians 4:2), and as I have often declared, "If you are having trouble with prayer, talk to God about it!"

In addition to the above, Luke gave a summary statement

of theses first few weeks of the early church: *"⁴³And awe came upon every soul, and many wonders and signs were being done through the apostles. ⁴⁴And all who believed were together and had all things in common. ⁴⁵And they were selling their possessions and belongings and distributing the proceeds to all, as any had need. ⁴⁶And day by day, attending the temple together and breaking bread in their homes, they received their food with glad and generous hearts, ⁴⁷praising God and having favor with all the people. And the Lord added to their number day by day those who were being saved"* (Acts 2:42-47).

We learn quite a few facts from that summary. Let us look at verse 43: *"Everyone kept feeling a sense of awe; and many wonders and signs were [or kept on] taking place through the apostles"* (Acts 2:43 NASB). The awe kept on coming and the wonders and signs kept on coming, just as they did in the ministry of Jesus.

The apostles did the wonders and signs; they had "power from on high" (Acts 1:8) and they exercised that power. *"Now many signs and wonders were regularly done among the people by the hands of the apostles"* (Acts 5:12). Much later we read *"And God was doing extraordinary miracles by the hands of Paul"* (Acts 19:11).

In addition, the sense of community was so strong that belongings were now of so little importance in their lives that they were being sold, and the money was given to those who had needs. Here we see the social work of the church commencing.

In addition, they kept the Jewish pattern of prayers at the temple, and fellowship in the homes with meals. Numbers are no longer being kept, as the Lord added to the church day by day new believers who had, after repentance, experienced salvation from their sins.

And out of all the "many wonders and signs" done by the apostles, God only revealed one incident to Luke to record in detail. That miracle and its impact occupies the next two chapters of Acts, chapters 3 and 4.

10

It Happened on the Way to Worship

There was much excitement on the Day of Pentecost and the following weeks. The record of one incident and its impact in chapter 3 continues through most of chapter 4. Why this one miracle out of the "many" of Acts 2:43? It is probably because there are valuable lessons to be learned here, and so we will spend time analyzing it. *"Now Peter and John were going up to the temple at the hour of prayer, the ninth hour [3 p.m.]"* (Acts 3:1).

Peter and John were of the Jewish faith, and they continued to attend the hours of prayer at the temple when they were in Jerusalem: 9 a.m., noon, and 3 p.m. (which they did "continually" Luke 24:53). We have already seen that the Day of Pentecost was a Jewish religious festival and the outpouring of God's power initially was only on Jewish followers of Jesus. Right up to chapter 13 the apostles attempted to reach people of the Jewish faith wherever they found them.

On Paul's journeys it seems he almost always went first to the local synagogue and attempted to share the good news. Even though Paul told the Jews that his team was *"turning to the Gentiles"* in Acts 13:46 after being rejected by the local Jews, he still visited the synagogue in Iconium, the next town he visited. And as late as chapter 21 Paul was willing to conform with the requirements of Judaism. These events took place long after the first Gentile experience of Pentecost had occurred in the house of Cornelius in Acts 10:44-46!

I really want to get to Acts 3:6, but I would be doing you a disservice if I omitted the clear teaching of these earlier verses. *"²And a man lame from birth was being carried, whom they laid daily at the gate of the temple that is called the Beautiful Gate to ask alms of those entering the temple. ³Seeing Peter and John about to go into the temple, he asked to receive alms"* (Acts 3:2-3). No doubt Peter and John talked as they went along, and because they had trodden this path three times a day for countless days, they would not have had to concentrate very much on what they were seeing. This walk could be called one of the "humdrum" activities of the day, a normal occurrence.

We can assume from the record that the lame man had been sitting at the Beautiful Gate for some years, and Peter and John had walked past him many times and had probably dropped coins into his hand. And yet, in this normal, everyday situation, on this particular day, guidance was given to Peter to tell the lame man to look at both of them. *"And Peter directed his gaze at him, as did John, and said, 'Look at us.'"* (verse 4).

Peter spoke to the lame man on that particular day because he was guided by God to do so. You too can watch for, expect, and perceive God's guidance throughout your day. Look for it in the small things of life, and then when you have a situation that looms large on the horizon, you will have confidence that guidance will be available just when you need it. I am convinced that God gives far more guidance than we will ever be conscious of.

Renew your mind to this truth by searching God's Word for statements and examples that demonstrate guidance. Put them into practice by thanking Him for showing you the best route to use to get where you want to go. And do not be misled by the fact that if a preacher indicates that this matter of guidance is one of "super spirituality." It is not. Guidance is yours for the taking moment by moment throughout the day. Get quiet, fix your mind on God, and be convinced that God has guidance for you. All this takes active, conscious effort, but the result is immeasurably worthwhile.

In a normal, everyday situation, guidance was given to Peter to tell the lame man at the gate of the temple to look at both of them. *"And Peter directed his gaze at him, as did John, and said, 'Look at us.'"* (Acts 3:4). The lame beggar was hoping for a monetary gift, but he got something greater. I found on the internet a sermon about this passage that Pastor Jerry Shirley had titled, "The Man Who Asked for Alms and Got Legs!"

"And he fixed his attention on them, expecting to receive something from them" (verse 5). The word translated "expecting" in verse 5 in many translations, is a different word from the positive expectation in Hebrews 11:1, *"Now faith is the substance of things expected."* The lame man was watching for their next move, but had no assurance. He was ready to receive a gift, but had no foundation to

make it a certainty. See my online article "Expectation: the Key to Believing God."

Peter had a temporary cash-flow problem; he had no coins in the pocket of his robe. We've all been there. As Sydney Smith wrote in the late 1700s, "Poverty of course is no disgrace to a man, but it is confoundedly inconvenient." Yet when you have Christ in you and your God supplies all your need according to His riches in glory, then you have to work hard to be poor. Just because you have no coins in your pocket on a particular day does not make you poor. Just look at what Peter did without money!

So even though Peter had no coins, he said, *"Such as I have give I thee"* (KJV). I just love the familiar flow of the KJV. Underline those words in your Bible. In contrast the ESV seems so bland: *"What I do have I give to you"* (ESV). There's a bit more life in the Message Bible: *"Peter said, 'I don't have a nickel to my name, but what I do have, I give you...'"*

Some believe that the verse proves the disciples were poor, but other passages disprove that. Following Jesus around Galilee were helpers. *"[40b]Among them were Mary Magdalene, and Mary the mother of James the younger and of Joses, and Salome. [41]When he was in Galilee, they had followed him and given him support"* (Mark 15:40b-41 NET). Wuest's translation says they were *"ministering to Him the necessities of life,"* which in today's vernacular means that they "picked up the tab." So, the traveling party of Jesus was well taken care of.

"Such as I have..." What did Peter have? That is the question that needs to be considered here, and the answer to that question is what you need to drill into your mind

constantly, hourly if necessary, until it is part of your being. Whatever Peter had, it worked! Paul encouraged the Corinthians to give money *"out of what you have"* (II Corinthians 8:11), because that was their responsibility. You can only give out of what you have.

And here in Acts 3 it was Peter's responsibility to give out of what he knew he had. Peter was not a model disciple of Jesus, yet he acted upon what he knew he had spiritually. Jesus had reminded his disciples on the night before he was crucified what he had taught them (see John chapters 14 to 16), so someone had been listening! He didn't yet know the "all truth" of John 16:13, as much of this came through the apostle Paul later, but he knew enough.

• Peter knew that he had he had the authority of Jesus Christ of Nazareth, the Christian's power of attorney, and he used it to perform this miracle (John 14:12, 15:16). He later explained this in Acts 3:16, and to the rulers and elders in Acts 4:10-12.

• Peter knew he had the Comforter in him (John 14:17), for he had been present on the Day of Pentecost; he had been *"clothed with,"* like a garment, *"with power from on high"*; truly spirit-filled; wall-to-wall with God's gift of the Holy Spirit!

• Peter knew he had Christ within him and he was in Christ (John 14:20). Peter may not have known the extent and greatness of the power of Christ's presence or of his own position in Christ, but he believed what Jesus said about them. For a Christian, "Such as I have..." is always better than money!

The recognition of all the possessions the believer has been given by God in Christ can be found in detail in the revelation Paul received, such as in Ephesians chapters 1 to 3, but that was a few decades ahead of this point of time. I have covered all this in my book *In Christ, Christ In*, so I will not repeat it here. In Christ I am accepted, secure, and significant. The point I would like to make is to read all of the book of Acts and marvel at what the early church did with the little they knew and without the detail that would follow in Paul's letters.

We could spend a lot of time exploring the teachings of Jesus to his disciples. Often he taught them that what was happening was to fulfill prophecy or was required by the law of Moses, yet on other occasions he taught the disciples in private what his parables really meant and what would happen in the future after his death. All of that would take a thick volume to discuss, and others have done so with distinction. As has been well said, only the truth you know will set you free (John 8:32).

Even then you don't need to know everything about the truth. For example, you don't need to know how electricity is produced; you only need to know how to make it work. Thank God you are well provided for as a believer, for God has set in the church "teachers" (Ephesians 4:11) and other ministries to help you.

Why don't we see these events regularly in the western world? Because we don't know what we have, having been "dumbed-down" by the preacher or denominational doctrine, or we just don't believe what we have. Paul's revelation later taught us that we should "put on Christ" in our minds (Romans 13:14, Galatians 3:27), that we have already "put on the new man" (Colossians 3:10), that we have all that God had promised the disciples, that we are blessed with every spiritual blessing in Christ (Ephesians 1:3). I have taught for six decades that you have all you need for every situation you will ever run across.

With the knowing comes responsibility. *"⁶Such as I have give I thee: In the name of Jesus Christ of Nazareth, rise up and walk!" (KJV) "⁷And he took him by the right hand and raised him up, and immediately his feet and ankles were made strong. ⁸And leaping up he stood and began to walk, and entered the temple with them, walking and leaping and praising God"* (Acts 3:6-8). Peter acted on the authority of the name of Jesus Christ and turned a 40-year-old (Acts 4:22) disabled beggar into a world-class hurdler!

The words "rise up" do not appear in all Greek manuscripts, so Peter could have said, "In the name of Jesus Christ of Nazareth, Walk!" In Greek grammar, "walk" is in the present imperative: "begin to walk and keep on walking." *"And he [Peter] took him by the right hand and raised him up, and immediately his feet and ankles were made strong"* (Acts 3:7). The lifting up by Peter was an encouragement to the man who may never have stood on the soles of his feet. I doubt Peter would have done it unless he had received a revelation from God.

This is an interesting parallel of the moment when Jesus had lifted Peter's mother-in-law to her feet and she was healed of a fever: *"And he came and took her by the hand and lifted her up, and the fever left her, and she began to serve them"* (Mark 1:31).

It is also similar to the healing of a lame man by Paul in Lystra in Acts 14:8-10. Interestingly, on that occasion we are specifically told that Paul saw (perceived) *"that he had faith to be made well"* (verse 9).

Now I'd like you to underline "immediately" or "instantly" in your Bible (verse 7). The Gospel of Luke and the Book of Acts, both written by Luke, use this Greek word 17 times out of the 19 times in the New Testament. While it is a different word from that used 17 times in the Gospel of Mark, particularly in the early chapters, there seems to be agreement that here in Acts it is a good translation.

Many of these usages have to do with healing miracles. I can only think of one healing in the Gospels that was a two-stage healing, and that was the blind man at Bethsaida who, after Jesus touched him, could only *"see men, but they look like trees, walking"* (Mark 8:24). On the second touch, he saw "everything clearly." Some sick people were instructed to obey certain commands, like the ten lepers who were to visit the priest and get official confirmation, or the blind man, who, after Jesus put mud in his eyes, was told that when he washed them in the pool of Siloam, he would see.

The truth to be observed here is how promptly God works on behalf of the believer. God only inhabits time to look after His children; in spirit everything is immediate, provided it has been stated as God's will. When future events are revealed in scripture, they will happen exactly on time every time. We may think God is late (like the Seventh Day Adventists in the "Great Disappointment" of 1844), but the problem is with our understanding, not with God. To Isaiah in the Old Testament God said, *"Before they call I will answer; while they are yet speaking I will hear"* (Isaiah 65:24). There is no nanosecond delay with our loving God.

You are right to be amazed at how good a God we have, as were the witnesses of this incident of the lame man. Let's go back to Acts 3. "*⁹And all the people saw him walking and praising God, ¹⁰and recognized him as the one who sat at the Beautiful Gate of the temple, asking for alms. And they were filled with wonder and amazement at what had happened to him. ¹¹While he clung to Peter and John, all the people, utterly astounded, ran together to them in the portico called Solomon's*" (Acts 3:9-11).

Peter, as on the Day of Pentecost, took this opportunity to preach the resurrection of Jesus (Acts 3:12-15), but first he explained that the man was not healed by the apostles' own power or holiness (verse 12): "*Why do you wonder at this, or why do you stare at us, as though by our own power or piety we have made him walk?*" This man was healed by faith in the Name of the resurrected Jesus, "*And his name—by faith in his name—has made this man strong whom you see and know, and the faith that is through Jesus has given the man this perfect health in the presence of you all*" (verse 16).

Note the "perfect health," "perfect soundness" (KJV), the only usage of that Greek word for "perfect" as a noun in the New Testament, and as an adjective twice (James 1:4 and I Thessalonians 5:23). Albert Barne's in his *Notes on the Bible* wrote: "It denotes 'integrity of parts, freedom from any defect'; and it here means that the cure was perfect and entire, or that he was completely restored to the use of his limbs."

This was certainly a faith healing, and faith requires an object. The object of a Christian's faith was given by Paul as "*the God and Father of our Lord Jesus Christ*"

(Ephesians 1:3). Here in Acts 3 it is *"faith in his [Jesus']
name"* and *"faith that is through Jesus."* So this is
unquestionably faith in the power and authority resident
in the Name of Jesus. A quick reading of the Gospels will
yield statements by Jesus, such as *"According to your faith,
let it be done to you"* and *"Your faith has made you whole."*

> Faith, mighty faith, the promise sees,
> And looks to that alone;
> Laughs at impossibilities,
> And cries, "It shall be done!"
> *(John Wesley, 1742).*

We were taught in Bible college that there is a difference
between "faith healing" and "divine healing." The
denomination preferred the term "divine healing" to separate
their theology from the metaphysical movement. However,
there was a strong Christian healing emphasis in the US
from the 1870s until the 1900s and they used the term
"faith-cure" and taught divine healing by faith in God.

In a history of the healing movement in a book such
as *The Ministry of Healing* by renowned Baptist minister
A.J. Gordon (online under Articles at www.PeterWade.com),
you will discover that while there was a continuous thread
of healing from the early church onward to the present
day, much of the New Age, Christian Science, and mind
religions practiced "faith healing" from the mid-1850s
onward. So all faith healing is not divine, but all divine
healing requires faith.

Peter used the opportunity to preach the good news
of the resurrection to the assembled crowd. He mentioned
the death of Jesus but put all the emphasis on the resurrection.

Gordon Lindsay, a Pentecostal preacher who became
William Branham's campaign manager in the 1940-50s,

wrote a book titled *World Evangelization Now by Healing and Miracles* (1951), and the impact of Pentecost is a good example of this principle at work. Lindsay also wrote the classic book *Bible Days Are Here Again* (1949).

T.L. Osborn proved it in third-world countries (his book *Healing the Sick* has also become a classic), while William Branham, Oral Roberts, Jack Coe, and A.A. Allen were prominent nationally across the U.S. in tent evangelism for three or more decades and wrote many books.

Peter again called for repentance in this sermon, as he had on the Day of Pentecost. About 5,000 men became believers (Acts 4:4) as a result of this miracle and the sermon that followed. A supernatural event followed by a proclamation of truth produced great results for the early church. However, this healing record is not over yet, as opposition is about to hit.

11

Ignorant and Unlearned Men

No, the chapter title is not a slogan from the feminist movement, but an important statement in our journey of exploration through Acts chapters 3-4.

In chapter 3 Peter and John healed the lame man in the Name of Jesus, who immediately began *"walking and leaping and praising God."* This caused quite a stir in the temple, as the lame beggar was well-known to the regular worshipers. The people *"were filled with wonder and amazement at what had happened to him"* (verse 10), so Peter took the opportunity to declare that the man had been healed *"by faith in his [Jesus'] Name."*

Peter made the point that the Jewish people had cried out for Jesus to be crucified, and he went straight on to proclaim the resurrection of Christ from the dead (Acts 3:15). The resurrection became the predominant message of good news given by the early church, and this is what caused the problem with the religious leaders of the day. Apart from this incident, there is very little in the book of Acts on "the message of the Cross," as some term the death of Jesus. However, *"with great power the apostles were giving their testimony to the resurrection of the Lord Jesus, and great grace was upon them all"* (Acts 4:33). Everyone dies, but there have only been a few resurrections, and apart from Jesus those resurrected later died again.

Due to all the commotion in the temple at the evening prayers, and because Peter again taught about the resurrection of the dead, the authorities acted. *"¹And as they were speaking to the people, the priests and the captain of the temple and the Sadducees came upon them, ²greatly annoyed because they were teaching the people and proclaiming in Jesus the resurrection from the dead. ³And they arrested them and put them in custody until the next day, for it was already evening"* (Acts 4:1-2).

The Sadducees were a sect within the Jewish faith who were anti-supernatural and did not believe in miraculous events like resurrections. That is why they were "sad, you see!" So they jailed Peter and John overnight to face the court in the morning, *"But many of those who had heard the word believed, and the number of the men came to about five thousand"* (Acts 4:4). There is some evidence that the "about five thousand" was the total number of Christians at that point, but not all see it that way.

The next morning Peter and John were given a top-level audience with the high priest and family, previous high priests, and also the Sanhedrin (70 leaders of the Jewish faith). *"And when they had set them* [and the former lame man] *in the midst, they inquired, 'By what power or by what name did you do this?'"* (verse 7). So there was no denial or question of the healing itself but rather a questioning of the "how." Peter, who had denied any association with Jesus just weeks before, was now a changed man, *"filled with the Holy Spirit"* (verse 8). Stand him up and he'd preach anywhere! So he laid into the Sanhedrin, the 70, who had insisted the Romans crucify Jesus. *"Let it be known to all of you and to all the people of Israel that by the name of Jesus Christ of Nazareth, whom you crucified, whom God raised from the dead—by him this man is standing before you well"* (verse 10).

Since the once-lame man was standing beside Peter and John (verse 14), tnese words were along the same line of "Now what have *you* got to say about *your* unbelief?" And next the salvation appeal to the 70 plus religious leaders, *"And there is salvation in no one else, for there is no other name under heaven given among men by which we must be saved"* (verse 12). In other words, "And *you* need to get saved also!" Don't you just love it? This is what pastors call "preaching to the choir."

Just as I love the familiar yet old-worldly flow of the KJV in Acts 3:6, *"Such as I have give I thee,"* I also love the KJV translation of Acts 4:13, *"Now when they saw the boldness of Peter and John, and perceived that they were **unlearned and ignorant men**, they marveled; and they took knowledge of them, that they had been with Jesus."* What a testimony from the opposition! Oh, how we need men like that today! The 70 leaders were all university or seminary graduates of their day, yet here were the deplorable country bumpkins from Galilee doing what the leaders could not do.

How often through history we have seen that God has mightily used "unlearned and ignorant" men. One I have already mentioned is William Branham. Born to a poorest of the poor family and with only elementary schooling in a one-room schoolhouse in Indiana, he received a visitation from God and was the forerunner of the healing evangelists of the 1940s onward. He had the truest gift of the word of knowledge and visions about people he would later meet wanting prayer for healing. Thousands flocked to his early meetings, and evangelists like Oral Roberts, T.L. Osborn, F.F. Bosworth and others held him in high esteem in his early ministry.

"Unlearned" actually means uninstructed in the professional rabbinical schools, just as Jesus was regarded, *"How is it that this man has learning, when he has never studied?"* (John 7:15). "Ignorant" is from the Greek word "idiot" which the English language borrowed, and really means "a man not in office, or a man who had not opportunities of education or accustomed to public speaking" (Barnes) and came to denote "those who are rude and illiterate." It was used of the common person in the street, the "hoi polloi," a lay person. They just didn't move in the same circles as rabbis, and the same is true of many Pentecostal preachers since the early 1900s who never studied to be ministers but just followed the calling of God on their lives.

"They recognized that they had been with Jesus" (ESV). This is obviously literal, in that someone in the Sanhedrin or temple guards had seen Peter and John in the company of Jesus. The overturning of the money-changers' tables and the preaching of Jesus in the temple area would make it obvious that the authorities were keeping watch on Jesus and his band of disciples.

However, there seems to be more in the statement that concerns their confidence and their actions. "Their whole being identified them with Jesus. 'We thought we had got rid of Him; but lo! He reappears in these men, and all that troubled us in the Nazarene Himself has yet to be put down in these His disciples.' What a testimony to these primitive witnesses! Would that the same could be said of their successors!" (Jamieson, Fausset and Brown).

So instead of the human Jesus, the Sanhedrin had two men standing before them with Christ in them and another 5,000 plus in the city of Jerusalem, all with Christ in them. *"But we impart a secret and hidden wisdom of God... None of the rulers of this age understood this, for if they had, they would not have crucified the Lord of glory"* (I Corinthians 2:7a,8). Now the religious leaders have a problem! *"But seeing the man who was healed standing beside them, they had nothing to say in opposition"* (Acts 4:14).

12

Great Power and Great Grace

Peter and John, in the Name of Jesus, healed the lame man at the gate of the Temple, and the crowd saw it and were amazed. Peter took the opportunity to tell the people about Jesus, and 5,000 men believed. But the temple guards arrested them both and they faced the Sanhedrin the next day, who *"took knowledge of [these unlearned and ignorant men], that they had been with Jesus"* (Acts 4:13 KJV).

We take up the record in verse 15. The religious authorities now had a problem! *"15But when they had commanded them to leave the council, they conferred with one another, 16saying, 'What shall we do with these men? For that a notable sign has been performed through them is evident to all the inhabitants of Jerusalem, and we cannot deny it. 17But in order that it may spread no further among the people, let us warn them to speak no more to anyone in this name'"* (Acts 4:15-17). The people who had seen the healing were their own "church members," as this happened on their own doorstep! As a result of Peter's teaching, thousands of men were added to the believers.

Rather than encourage the presence of God in their

midst, they didn't like the concept that power was in "the Name of Jesus" rather than in the authority of the Jewish faith. And being Sadducees they did not want to see the supernatural in action and everyone getting excited, rather than acting humble and worshiping quietly. These attitudes have persisted to the present day.

One time when I was teaching in upstate New York in the United States, I had a phone call from a pastor, as some of his members had been invited by a friend of mine to hear me speak. He boldly asked me what I was going to speak about—I was on his turf and he was concerned about his authority as a pastor. I was tempted to reply "about God and about 20 minutes," which is an old joke between my wife Vivien and me about what to teach next Sunday. I was gracious to him, and didn't take the opportunity to point out his own insecurity that prompted the question. I could have quoted scripture like "what is that to thee?" (John 21:22 KJV), but I didn't.

So Peter and John were brought before the authorities again and they "*18charged them not to speak or teach at all in the name of Jesus. 19But Peter and John answered them, 'Whether it is right in the sight of God to listen to you rather than to God, you must judge, 20for we cannot but speak of what we have seen and heard.'*" (Acts 4:18-20). This was the "boldness" of Peter and John that verse 13 spoke about. They simply did what God guided them to do, and they were going to keep on doing it.

"*21And when they had further threatened them, they let them go, finding no way to punish them, because of the people, for all were praising God for what had happened. 22For the man on whom this sign of healing was performed was more than forty years old.* [23] *When they were released, they went to their friends and reported what the chief priests and the elders had said to them"* (Acts 4:21-23).

The believers then took the situation to God in prayer. *"*[29]*And now, Lord, look upon their threats and grant to your servants to continue to speak your word with all boldness,* [30]*while you stretch out your hand to heal, and signs and wonders are performed through the name of your holy servant Jesus"* (Acts 29-30). Two important keys in the book of Acts to power that impacts lives are right there: speak God's Word with boldness, and meet people's needs in the authority of the Name of Jesus. With the indwelling spirit of God, they had all the strength and wisdom they needed to speak the Word and act on the Word.

Note that boldness doesn't imply shouting, and shouting does not indicate anointing. Boldness is saying what God wants to be said regardless of who is listening. I change television channels when someone is shouting at me. Shouting while preaching is more often a sign that the argument being made is weak. I'm sure some preachers have a side-note in their outline which says "shout here" or "cry here!" Someone went as far as saying "All preaching is yelling and all teaching is telling;" obviously spoken by a teacher! True preaching is proclaiming and true teaching is explaining.

God acknowledged their prayer by a special miracle. *"And when they had prayed, the place in which they were gathered together was shaken, and they were all filled with the Holy Spirit and continued to speak the word of God with boldness"* (verse 31). What a marvelous token of God's presence and power! We need more "place-shaking prayer" today, especially when it concerns governments and church powers. *"And with great power the apostles were giving their testimony to the resurrection of the Lord Jesus, and great grace* [favor] *was upon them all"* (verse 33). So the apostles continued doing what Jesus had told them to do.

13

Believers Helping Each Other

Acts chapter 5 should start at what is now Acts 4:34, as it introduces the circumstances that led to the incident involving Ananias and Sapphira. (This is an incident that those who want to return to the ways of the early church might not want to see repeated!) But since it doesn't start a new chapter in any Bible version, we are stuck with the convention.

"*34There was not a needy person among them, for as many as were owners of lands or houses sold them and brought the proceeds of what was sold 35and laid it at the apostles' feet, and it was distributed to each as any had need*" (Acts 4:34-35). There is no record of the apostles requesting people to sell their investment properties. This was not communism as we know it today. Gifts were distributed according to need—not to make all personal income equal, or all possessions belong to the state (a failed system that is being replaced by capitalism.)

The Old Testament law taught that the poor should be cared for and helped, and Jesus said, "*For you always have the poor with you*" (Matthew 26:11). "*But if anyone has the world's goods and sees his brother in need, yet closes his heart against him, how does God's love abide in him?"* (I John 3:17). It was and still is the right thing to look after the welfare of the poor. The verses in the first paragraph above follow the previous mention in Acts 2:44-45: *"And all who believed were together and had all things in common. ⁴⁵And they were selling their possessions and belongings and distributing the proceeds to all, as any had need"* and also verse 32 above, *"Now the full number of those who believed were of one heart and soul, and no one said that any of the things that belonged to him was his own, but they had everything in common."*

It has been suggested that since the priests were opposed to the believers, they deliberately ignored the poor Christians and gave them no practical help, so the believers "stepped up to the plate" and to this day the church universal helps meet the need of the less fortunate. In India, for example, where the gospel of grace has been taught for many centuries, only 2.3% of the population claim to be Christian, yet the vast majority of the hospitals and clinics are owned and operated by churches or Christian organizations. Even in Western nations there is an obvious presence of Christian-based medical care.

Now in the life of the early church we contiue to see some social work, and we are given two examples of believers who sold their investments in order to finance the social outreach of the church. *"³⁶Thus Joseph, who was also called by the apostles Barnabas (which means son of encouragement), a Levite, a native of Cyprus, ³⁷sold a field that belonged to him and brought the money and laid it at the apostles' feet"* (Acts 4:36-37). Barnabas later became a companion of Paul on his first missionary journey. This is just one example selected from many to demonstrate how the church was able to meet the needs of the poor.

A second example follows: *"¹But a man named Ananias, with his wife Sapphira, sold a piece of property, ²and with his wife's knowledge he kept back for himself some of the proceeds and brought only a part of it and laid it at the apostles' feet"* (Acts 5:1-2). This chapter has the first and last mention of Ananias and Sapphira, and we shall see why in the next few verses.

Peter, presumably by a word of knowledge from God, became aware of their deception and called Ananias to account for it. *"³But Peter said, 'Ananias, why has Satan filled your heart to lie to the Holy Spirit and to keep back for yourself part of the proceeds of the land? ⁴While it remained unsold, did it not remain your own? And after it was sold, was it not at your disposal? Why is it that you have contrived this deed in your heart? You have not lied to men but to God'"* (Acts 5:3-4). A good question, Peter, and we certainly would like to know the answer, but it was not to be forthcoming. Ananias had made out that his offering was the total amount from the property sale.

How did Ananias open the door of his heart to Satan and for what purpose? Did he just want to make a grand display of his benevolence to the apostles? It was a freewill offering, as Peter clearly indicated. However, Ananias didn't even have a chance to say "Guilty as charged." *"⁵When Ananias heard these words, he fell down and breathed his last. And great fear came upon all who heard of it. ⁶The young men rose and wrapped him up and carried him out and buried him"* (Acts 5:5-6).

It appears no-one went to find his wife Sapphira and tell her she was now a widow, perhaps because of the "great fear" that came upon the witnesses. It was three hours later when Sapphira finally came to Peter, ready to do what she and Ananias had agreed upon.

"*⁷After an interval of about three hours his wife came in, not knowing what had happened. ⁸And Peter said to her, 'Tell me whether you sold the land for so much.' And she said, 'Yes, for so much.' ⁹But Peter said to her, 'How is it that you have agreed together to test the Spirit of the Lord? Behold, the feet of those who have buried your husband are at the door, and they will carry you out.' ¹⁰Immediately she fell down at his feet and breathed her last. When the young men came in they found her dead, and they carried her out and buried her beside her husband. ¹¹And great fear came upon the whole church and upon all who heard of these things*" (Acts 5:7-11).

So we see a new example of the manifestation of the power of God. A godly life is based upon truth, not the praise of humans. I am not a believer in numbered envelopes for giving, like my church did when I was growing up. Nor am I a believer that the pastor or church board should prepare your tax return, as one Pentecostal preacher did in Australia.

The amount you give is your business, that only you and God should know. If in doubt, ask God for guidance. And if prayer is a problem to you, talk to God about it! But never make a display of your giving. Verse 11, by the way, is the first usage of the word "church" to describe the group of believers in the resurrected Christ.

Do you remember the poor widow in the gospel of

Mark who gave all she had? "*⁴¹And he [Jesus] sat down opposite the treasury and watched the people putting money into the offering box. Many rich people put in large sums. ⁴²And a poor widow came and put in two small copper coins* [mites, KJV], *which make a penny. ⁴³And he called his disciples to him and said to them, "Truly, I say to you, this poor widow has put in more than all those who are contributing to the offering box. ⁴⁴For they all contributed out of their abundance, but she out of her poverty has put in everything she had, all she had to live on."* (Mark 12:41-44). We are not told how it turned out for her, but a sanctified imagination who knows how to live in the flow of God's supply would say that God met all her need according to His riches in glory.

14

The Shadow of Peter

As we continue our journey through the first months of the life of the early church, we come to another summary of their activities. *"12Now many signs and wonders were regularly done among the people by the hands of the apostles. And they were all together in Solomon's Portico. 13None of the rest dared join them, but the people held them in high esteem"* (Acts 5:12-13).

In verse 12 *"the hands of the apostles"* are specifically mentioned. They are mentioned also in Acts 6:6 concerning healing, and in many other places concerning receiving the gift of the Holy Spirit. In the first detailed healing recorded after Pentecost, in Acts chapter 3, Peter commanded the man *"In the name of Jesus Christ of Nazareth, rise up and walk!"* and then *"took him by the right hand and raised him up"* (Acts 3:6-7). Perhaps in that case Peter could have been encouraging the man to act with faith. Now we see an indication that the laying on of hands is becoming a regular practice in the early church. It also indicates a divine-human reciprocity where man makes the first move as a faith action and God then moves to produce the miracle.

When Peter walked on water in Matthew 14:28-29, the record says "*²⁸And Peter answered him, 'Lord, if it is you, command me to come to you on the water.' ²⁹He said, 'Come.' So Peter got out of the boat and walked on the water and came to Jesus.*" Before the miracle could happen, Peter had to first step over the gunwhale (edge) of the boat; he had to take an action.

When God was training Moses to visit Pharoah, "*²The Lord said to him, 'What is that in your hand?' He said, 'A staff.' ³And he said, 'Throw it on the ground.' So he threw it on the ground, and it became a serpent, and Moses ran from it. ⁴But the Lord said to Moses, 'Put out your hand and catch it by the tail'—so he put out his hand and caught it, and it became a staff in his hand*" (Exodus 4:2-4). Man had to make the move (and a brave man at that!).

For further illustration I could add the making of wine by the servants pouring water at the command of Jesus in John chapter 2, the blind man who had to wash in the pool of Siloam and was healed in John chapter 9, the many wonders and signs which were done through (by in the KJV) the apostles in Acts 2:43. I could also point to Stephen, who in Acts 6 did great signs and wonders among the people, and of Paul and his companions at Iconium in Acts 14, where the Lord granted signs and wonders to be done by their hands. In the same chapter, Paul told a crippled man at Lystra to stand on his feet, and the man sprang up and walked! When the people saw "*what Paul had done*" they thought he was a god.

God made the promises, and man must make the first move to receive them. So in Acts 5 the same principle we saw at work in the Old Testament and the Gospels was still working, and continues to do so today.

In Acts 5:13 we read, *"None of the rest dared join them, but the people held them in high esteem."* Trying to discover the identity of "the rest" is the difficulty here. They are obviously not from the common people who were seeing family and friends receive healing. A few commentators say "the rest" are "the 'rich' men or the people of authority and influence among the Jews, of whom Ananias was one, and that they were deterred from it by the fate of Ananias" (Barnes). However, most commentaries wisely fail to comment! Your guess is as good as mine at this point.

"14And more than ever believers were added to the Lord, multitudes of both men and women, 15so that they even carried out the sick into the streets and laid them on cots and mats, that as Peter came by at least his shadow might fall on some of them. 16The people also gathered from the towns around Jerusalem, bringing the sick and those afflicted with unclean spirits, and they were all healed" (Acts 5:14-16).

Growth continued and numbers were no longer estimated, as "multitudes" of believers were added "to the Lord." In a church today, an event like the sudden demise of Ananias and Sapphira because of a lie would have caused an exodus! But the signs and wonders were the best form of advertising and evangelism, and when people are getting help, they tell others, who then flock to the source to get their needs met also. In the mid-1940s through to the 1960s this happened to nationally known healing evangelists in the US. Auditoriums of those days were rarely big enough to hold the crowds, so the evangelists purchased tents, one of which seated up to 20,000 people.

We now read that people *"even carried out the sick into the streets and laid them on cots and mats, that as Peter came by at least his shadow might fall on some of them"* (Acts 5:15). The record does not say that people were healed because Peter's shadow fell on them. Charismatics might like to think so, but it is more likely that because Peter had healed so many people, they even believed that perhaps his shadow would heal them.

In Acts 19:12 handkerchiefs and aprons were touched by Paul and then taken to sick people, *"and their diseases left them and the evil spirits came out of them."* We cannot limit how God works, so while there is no doubt in the Word about the effectiveness of Paul's method in Acts 19, there has to be a reason why there is no mention of anyone being healed when Peter's shadow passed over the infirm.

"The people also gathered from the towns around Jerusalem, bringing the sick and those afflicted with unclean spirits, and they were all healed" (Acts 5:16). Perhaps it is time I should make special mention of the "all" in so many verses in the early chapters of the book of Acts, as well as in the Gospel records. Strong's Concordance defines the word as "absolutely *all* or (singular) *every* one." I have been saying for decades that you can study Greek until you are blue in the face, but "all" will still mean "all." This is true of "all" or "every" so long as they are not modified by other words, for example, "all children" or "every priest." In this text, there is no doubt shown that any missed out on their deliverance. *"They were all healed."*

Unfortunately this is not seen in the present day and leads some to theorize about whether it was God's will or not to be healed, or the fault of the person being ministered to, or perhaps the preacher's fault that someone was not healed. I read of how Oral Roberts came close to quitting his healing ministry because not every one he ministered to showed immediate signs of improvement. He finally resolved the issue by reporting that God had said to him that Oral's job was to lay his hands on the sick, and it was God's business whether they were healed immediately or later.

Some students of the Word point to the man who came to Jesus for healing in Mark chapter 8. "*22And they came to Bethsaida. And some people brought to him a blind man and begged him to touch him. 23And he took the blind man by the hand and led him out of the village, and when he had spit on his eyes and laid his hands on him, he asked him, 'Do you see anything?'. 24And he looked up and said, 'I see men, but they look like trees, walking.'. 25Then Jesus laid his hands on his eyes again; and he opened his eyes, his sight was restored, and he saw everything clearly*" (Mark 8:22-24). "This is the single case of a gradual cure in the healings wrought by Jesus. The reason for this method in this case is not given" (Robertson's Word Pictures). However, the "gradual cure" only took seconds. So the "why" in this incident is not a case where a public explanation has to be given. There is no benefit in pursuing the issue when the Word is silent.

15

The Words of This Life

The second persecution of the apostles now occurs. The patience of the High Priest seems to have run out, as healings and signs and wonders continue all over Jerusalem. *"¹⁷But the high priest rose up, and all who were with him (that is, the party of the Sadducees), and filled with jealousy ¹⁸they arrested the apostles and put them in the public prison"* (Acts 5:17-18). He might have been a high priest in the Jewish religion, but he obviously had not yet learned the lesson God gave him during the first persecution in Acts chapters 3 and 4. So, God does something spectacular to catch his attention.

"¹⁹But during the night an angel of the Lord opened the prison doors and brought them out, and said, ²⁰"Go and stand in the temple and speak to the people all the words of this Life" (Acts 5:19-20). Here we have words sent directly from the throne of God and delivered by an angel. Preachers and teachers today should take note! The world needs to hear "The words of This Life," not "Seven Steps to Debt Destruction" or "Daniel: The Key to the Book of Revelation." Verse 20 is one of my favorite verses... "all the words of this Life" (KJV and many others). A

"beautiful expression for that Life in the Risen One which was the burden of their preaching!" (JFB commentary).

The "words of this Life" does not refer to the Apostles' Creed or the Articles of Faith of your fellowship. A number of translations capitalize the word "Life" to indicate that it was the resurrection life of Christ resident in the apostles since the Day of Pentecost that they were to speak about. The apostles had demonstrated that they had the authority of the Name of Jesus, they had the constant presence of the Comforter within, and they were learning what it meant when Jesus said, *"you in me and I in you"* (John 14:20 ESV).

The people in Jerusalem knew it was not a case of "easy believism" to follow Christ, because after the Ananias and Sapphira incident and the following miracles, *"none of those who were not of their number dared to join and associate with them, but the people held them in high regard and praised and made much of them"* (Acts 5:13 AMP). There was a cultural and religious price to pay to be a believer in the resurrection of Jesus, just as there is today in Muslim-controlled countries. I remind you of the teaching by Jesus on the bread of life, and *"after this many of his disciples turned back and no longer walked with him"* (John 6:66).

> Sing them over again to me,
> Wonderful words of life,
> Let me more of their beauty see,
> Wonderful words of life;
> Words of life and beauty
> Teach me faith and duty.
> Beautiful words, wonderful words,
> Wonderful words of life.
>
> *(Philip P. Bliss, 1874).*

The apostles put great emphasis on the Resurrection of Christ (see chapter 17 below). This command by the angel of the Lord should be on every preacher's desk! *"Tell the people everything there is to say about this Life"* (MSG). *"Tell the people everything about life in Christ"* (God's Word). Which is exactly what the apostles did.

"²¹And when they heard this, they entered the temple at daybreak and began to teach. Now when the high priest came, and those who were with him, they called together the council and all the senate of the people of Israel and sent to the prison to have them brought. ²²But when the officers came, they did not find them in the prison, so they returned and reported, ²³'We found the prison securely locked and the guards standing at the doors, but when we opened them we found no one inside'" (Acts 5:21-23).

Hah! I won't be presumptuous and put words into the mouth of God, but I would have said, "How about that, O Great High Priest. I just want you to know that I'm working here!" I just love it when God sends a personal message through the display of His power.

"²⁴Now when the captain of the temple and the chief priests heard these words, they were greatly perplexed about them, wondering what this would come to. ²⁵And someone came and told them, 'Look! The men whom you put in prison are standing in the temple and teaching the people.' ²⁶Then the captain with the officers went and brought them, but not by force, for they were afraid of being stoned by the people" (Acts 5:24-26).

The captain and officers were probably from the temple guards, religious men but in fear of being set upon by the inhabitants of Jerusalem. Peter and the apostles had been down this road before, and were glad of another opportunity to speak "the words of this Life" to the highest religious figures in the land. While they probably knew that they would not change the high priest's mind, they did know that he and his inner circle were without excuse in God's sight.

"*27And when they had brought them, they set them before the council. And the high priest questioned them, 28saying, 'We strictly charged you not to teach in this name, yet here you have filled Jerusalem with your teaching, and you intend to bring this man's blood upon us.' 29But Peter and the apostles answered,'We must obey God rather than men.'*" So there's the answer to your first charge, High Priest. The same one we gave you last time we met! And as to our teaching, here it is again: "*'30The God of our fathers raised Jesus, whom you killed by hanging him on a tree. 31God exalted him at his right hand as Leader and Savior, to give repentance to Israel and forgiveness of sins. 32And we are witnesses to these things, and so is the Holy Spirit, whom God has given to those who obey him'*" Acts 5:27-32).

Notice that the apostles claimed to be witnesses to the death and resurrection of Christ. This they were, this they preached, this is what stuck in the craw of the Sadducees, who did not believe in the supernatural. And the Holy Spirit was witness to both the death and resurrection, as well as to Christ's seating at the right hand of God (verse 31). And in this second trial, the apostles' candor and fearlessness made the council so angry that they wanted to kill them right then and there. "*And when they heard that, they were cut to the heart, and took counsel to slay them"* (Acts 5:33). *"When they heard that, they were furious and wanted to kill them on the spot"* (MSG).

At last some wisdom

"34But a Pharisee in the council named Gamaliel, a teacher of the law held in honor by all the people, stood up and gave orders to put the men outside for a little while. 35And he said to them, 'Men of Israel, take care what you are about to do with these men. 36For before these days Theudas rose up, claiming to be somebody, and a number of men, about four hundred, joined him. He was killed, and all who followed him were dispersed and came to nothing. 37After him Judas the Galilean rose up in the days of the census and drew away some of the people after him. He too perished, and all who followed him were scattered. 38So in the present case I tell you, keep away from these men and let them alone, for if this plan or this undertaking is of man, it will fail; 39but if it is of God, you will not be able to overthrow them. You might even be found opposing God!'" (Acts 5:34-39a).

Just to clear the air, the Theudas mentioned in verse 36 is not the same Theudas mentioned by Josephus in his book *The Antiquities of the Jews, Book XX, chapter V,* written some 10 years later. Josephus does mention Judas the Galilean.

"You might even be found fighting against God!" (verse 39, AMP) seems to suggest that Gamaliel, as a Pharisee, had some sympathy for the apostles, as Pharisees believed in supernatural events. To oppose God is to put your own position on the line, so the Sadducees yielded to the advise from the opposing party.

[39b]*"So they took his advice,* [40]*and when they had called in the apostles, they beat them and charged them not to speak in the name of Jesus, and let them go.* [41]*Then they left the presence of the council, rejoicing that they were counted worthy to suffer dishonor for the name"* (Acts 39b-41). To "beat" the apostles is to "flay" them, also known as flogging, lashing, or scourging. This was common in Roman times, regardless of whether the unfortunate person had yet to be tried. So it was a vindictive action, much like a clip around the ear by the local policeman in my childhood, which got results then, but would cause an early retirement for him today. It was, however, the first recorded time the apostles had gone through the experience, and was no doubt very painful.

"[42]And every day, in the temple and from house to house, they did not cease teaching and preaching Jesus as the Christ" (Acts 5:41-42). Whenever and wherever an opportunity arose, they taught and preached. I've often said, "Stand me up at the front and I'll teach the Word every time," because that is what I've been called to do, and I'm in good company.

And another summary of the momentum of the early church is given in the next chapter, *"And the word of God continued to increase, and the number of the disciples multiplied greatly in Jerusalem, and a great many of the priests became obedient to the faith"* (Acts 6:7). The word *increased* and the disciples *multiplied*—a lovely expressive emphasis on the rapid growth. The High Priest could not even control the hungry hearts of the priests for the truth. And even today we need lots of preachers to come to a saving knowledge of the Lord Jesus Christ.

16

The First Deacons and the First Martyr

Acts chapter 6 starts with another church business meeting in the Congregational style. *"¹Now in these days when the disciples were increasing in number, a complaint by the Hellenists arose against the Hebrews because their widows were being neglected in the daily distribution. ²And the twelve summoned the full number of the disciples and said, 'It is not right that we should give up preaching the word of God to serve tables. ³Therefore, brothers, pick out from among you seven men of good repute, full of the Spirit and of wisdom, whom we will appoint to this duty. ⁴But we will devote ourselves to prayer and to the ministry of the word'"* (Acts 6:1-4).

Hellenists or Grecians (KJV) were Greek-speaking Jews who lived in Jerusalem but came from other countries. The Twelve were determined not to swerve from their mission as preachers of the Word and "witnesses to the resurrection," so they asked for seven nominations from the whole congregation and then appointed them as deacons "over this duty" ("business," KJV).

"The ministry [Greek word is deacons] *of the word"*

and now we have deacons of the business, preaching elders and business elders. This was in the Jewish tradition as every synagogue had a rabbi (the teacher) and three deacons who were judges of sacred and civil matters. It is yet another evidence that the majority of Christian believers were practicing Jews and as such, law-keepers.

One of the appointed deacons was Stephen. *"⁵And what they said pleased the whole gathering, and they chose Stephen, a man full of faith and of the Holy Spirit, and Philip, and Prochorus, and Nicanor, and Timon, and Parmenas, and Nicolaus, a proselyte of Antioch. ⁶These they set before the apostles, and they prayed and laid their hands on them. ⁷And the word of God continued to increase, and the number of the disciples multiplied greatly in Jerusalem, and a great many of the priests became obedient to the faith. ⁸And Stephen, full of grace and power, was doing great wonders and signs among the people"* (Acts 6:5-8). Apart from Stephen and Philip, all we know of the other five deacons is recorded here.

The record now picks up the actions of several synagogues in Jerusalem who *"could not withstand the wisdom and the Spirit with which he was speaking"* (Acts 6:10). They set up false witnesses to lie about him, who said, *"This man never ceases to speak words against this holy place and the law, for we have heard him say that this Jesus of Nazareth will destroy this place and will change the customs that Moses delivered to us"* (Acts 6:13-14), which led to the trial of Stephen.

In the trial, *"And gazing at him, all who sat in the council saw that his face was like the face of an angel"* (Acts 6:15). *"¹And the high priest said, "Are these things* so?" *2And Stephen said: "Brothers and fathers, hear me"* (Acts 7:1-2). There is much to be gained by reading Stephen's sermon in Acts 7:2-53. The trial ended in Stephen's martyrdom by stoning, *"And the witnesses laid down their garments at the feet of a young man named Saul"* (Acts 7:58), later to be renamed Paul.

"1And Saul approved of his execution. And there arose on that day a great persecution against the church in Jerusalem, and they were all scattered throughout the regions of Judea and Samaria, except the apostles. 2Devout men buried Stephen and made great lamentation over him. 3But Saul was ravaging the church, and entering house after house, he dragged off men and women and committed them to prison" (Acts 8:1-3.)

Here for the present I'm going to conclude our journey through the first two years of the early church. It has been a powerful time for those who were involved, and for those of us who look back on it for inspiration and example. You will gain much more insight if you read the book of Acts and this book again. It is really amazing how much you will pick up on your second reading.

Next I want to share for you why the Apostles were so adamant to continue preaching the resurrection of Jesus, when it was the very topic causing all the persecution.

17
Why Emphasize the Resurrection?

Both the historical record of the early church in Acts and the letters of Paul place the emphasis of their preaching on the Resurrection of Christ. They do mention the death of Jesus on the cross and his burial, but we as Christian believers are to look at the other side of the cross as well! Speaking of resurrection from the dead, Paul writes *"And if Christ hasn't been made to live, your faith is a hollow shell and you're still a bunch of sinners"* (I Corinthians 15:14 Cotton Patch Version).

Maybe you'd prefer the Message Bible paraphrase, *"And face it—if there's no resurrection for Christ, everything we've told you is smoke and mirrors, and everything you've staked your life on is smoke and mirrors."* Regardless of which translation or paraphrase you read, without the resurrection of Christ there is no Christian life and *"we are of all men most miserable"* (verse 19 KJV)!

So on the basis of the above verses in I Corinthians 15, I think we can discount the theory that Peter and later Paul were merely trying to annoy the Sadducees, who did not believe in angels, spirit, or resurrection. The Twelve were witnesses of the resurrection and nothing was going to stop them from telling people what they had seen.

On the Day of Pentecost, Peter preached the first public sermon of the Christian church. After recounting the life and death of Jesus (Acts 2:23), he proclaimed that *"God raised him up, loosing the pangs of death, because it was not possible for him to be held by it"* (verse 24). *"This Jesus God raised up, and of that we all are witnesses... Let all the house of Israel therefore know for certain that God has made him both Lord and Christ, this Jesus whom you crucified"* (verses 32, 36). About three thousand people were added to the church that day. Preach it, brother!

Then in chapter 3 we have the record of Peter and John going up to the temple to pray probably a week or so later, and the lame man was healed. Peter didn't miss the opportunity to preach the resurrection to the people again. On this occasion the priests were *"greatly annoyed because they were teaching the people and proclaiming in Jesus the resurrection from the dead"* (Acts 4:2). Peter and John were arrested and got to spend the night in custody, but in the meantime *"many of those who had heard the word believed, and the number of the men came to about five thousand"* (verse 4). Another great result from proclaiming the resurrection of Christ!

After being released, they organized a prayer meeting with all the believers. They prayed to be able to continue *"to speak the word of God with boldness"* (verse 31), after being commanded *"not to speak at all nor teach in the name of Jesus"* (verse 18). *"And with great power the apostles were giving their testimony to the resurrection of the Lord Jesus, and great grace was upon them all"* (verse 33). The "great power" was resident within them because they had received the gift of the Holy Spirit, and with it came "great grace."

In the next chapter, after another imprisonment that failed when an angel came at night and opened the doors (Acts 5:19-20), Peter and the apostles went to the temple the next day. Yet again they taught the people and they were hauled before the Sanhedrin and the high priest. Peter and other apostles answered the charges with, *"31God exalted* [lifted up, Moffatt] *him at his right hand as Leader and Savior, to give repentance to Israel and forgiveness of sins. 32And we are witnesses to these things, and so is the Holy Spirit, whom God has given to those who obey him"* (verses 31-32).

In Acts 10, Peter was led of God to journey to Joppa and find the house of Simon the tanner. He was still preaching the resurrection of Jesus: *"40But God raised him on the third day and made him to appear, 41not to all the people but to us who had been chosen by God as witnesses, who ate and drank with him after he rose from the dead. 42And he commanded us to preach to the people and to testify that he is the one appointed by God to be judge of the living and the dead"* (verses 40-42).

Years later, on Paul's first missionary journey, Paul was preaching the resurrection of Jesus in the Jewish synagogue in a town named Antioch in Pisidia. *"30But God raised him from the dead, 31and for many days he appeared to those who had come up with him from Galilee to Jerusalem, who are now his witnesses to the people... 34And as for the fact that he raised him from the dead, no more to return to corruption, he has spoken in this way..."*

(Acts 13:30,31,34) and proceeded to quote David's messianic prophecies from the Psalms and other prophecies. So, Paul continued preaching the core message of the early church.

Then on Paul's second missionary journey, in Athens the people said of Paul, "*18And some said, 'What does this babbler [with his scrap-heap learning, AMP] wish to say?' Others said, 'He seems to be a preacher of foreign divinities'—because he was preaching Jesus and the resurrection*" (Acts 17:18). "*32Now when they heard of the resurrection of the dead, some mocked. But others said, 'We will hear you again about this'*" (verse 32).

Paul even used the resurrection as a defense tactic to divide the opposition when he was arrested yet again. "*6Now when Paul perceived that one part were Sadducees and the other Pharisees, he cried out in the council, "Brothers, I am a Pharisee, a son of Pharisees. It is with respect to the hope and the resurrection of the dead that I am on trial'*" (Acts 23:6). And it worked!

"*7And when he had said this, a dissension arose between the Pharisees and the Sadducees, and the assembly was divided. 8For the Sadducees say that there is no resurrection, nor angel, nor spirit, but the Pharisees acknowledge them all. 9Then a great clamor arose, and some of the scribes of the Pharisees' party stood up and contended sharply, 'We find nothing wrong in this man. What if a spirit or an angel spoke to him?' 10And when the dissension became violent, the tribune, afraid that Paul would be torn to pieces by them, commanded the soldiers to go down and take him away from among them by force and bring him into the barracks*" (Acts 23:7-10).

I'll leave it to you to read the whole of I Corinthians

chapter 15. *"³For I delivered to you as of first importance what I also received: that Christ died for our sins in accordance with the Scriptures, ⁴that he was buried, that he was raised on the third day in accordance with the Scriptures"* (verses 3-4), and then follow Paul's revelation of the believers' personal resurrection in Christ.

18

Acts and Receiving the Gift

As should be obvious to the readers of this book, speaking in tongues is not the primary focus of Pentecost. However, a final summary will provide a deeper understanding of this experience, especially to those believers who have laid aside tradition and prejudice and are ready to manifest speaking in tongues in their lives.

The devotional aspect of speaking in tongues in personal prayer is not mentioned in Acts. No doubt this is because it is private by its nature. You will have to read the three detailed chapters on spiritual gifts or manifestations in I Corinthians chapters 12 to 14 to understand its usage and its power. However, I am convinced it was used by believers during the Acts period because of the accepted date of the writing of I Corinthians.

The ESV Study Bible states "it is unclear whether this was the spring of A.D. 53, 54 or 55... near the end of his three-year ministry in Ephesus" (Acts 20:17, 31, I Corinthians 16:5-8). This would be in the closing stages of Paul's third missionary journey.

The detailed description of the correct usage of speaking in tongues in I Corinthians therefore overlaps some eight chapters of Acts, and seeks to correct the misuse of an experience that was by then a well-established feature of church life and private life of the believers in Corinth. Again, there is no reference in Acts of speaking in tongues in the common life of the fellowship. Acts does, however, give five reports of people receiving "the gift of the Holy Spirit," and these I will now address in the one place.

The Day of Pentecost

Acts 2:1-4 records the Day of Pentecost reception in the temple precinct in Jerusalem. On that occasion there were the special signs of the *"sound like a mighty rushing wind"* (verse 2), and the *"divided tongues as of fire"* that appeared to them and rested on each of them (verse 3). These signs were never repeated in the Acts records. Following the signs, the Twelve apostles *"were all filled with the Holy Spirit and began to speak in other tongues as the Spirit gave them utterance"* (verse 4).

The Spirit supplied the words; the apostles did the speaking. "It is next to certain that the speakers themselves understood nothing of what they uttered" (Jamieson, Fausset and Brown). *"As the Spirit kept giving them clear and loud expression [in each tongue in appropriate words]"* (AMP). *"And at this sound the multitude came together, and they were bewildered, because each one was hearing them speak in his own language"* (Acts 2:6). My earlier chapters go through this event in detail.

City of Samaria

The second experience is in Acts 8:14-23, and is the one the doubters emphasize because the words "speaking in tongues" do not appear. "*14Now when the apostles at Jerusalem heard that Samaria had received the word of God* [verse 12], *they sent to them Peter and John, 15who came down and prayed for them that they might receive the Holy Spirit, 16for he had not yet fallen on any of them, but they had only been baptized in the name of the Lord Jesus. 17Then they laid their hands on them and they received the Holy Spirit"* (Acts 8:14-17). Since no one laid their hands on the Twelve on the Day of Pentecost, the prayer and laying on of hands are new actions of which no explanation is given.

However, what is important is verse 18: *"Now when Simon saw that the Spirit was given through the laying on of the apostles' hands..."* Obviously Simon must have not only seen the laying on of hands but also heard something. Adam Clarke, Albert Barnes, John Gill, and many others (who were not charismatics), write in their commentaries that speaking in tongues must have been heard by Simon. A.T. Robinson, in his *Word Pictures*, writes concerning the word "saw": "This participle (second aorist active of *horao*) shows plainly that those who received the gift of the Holy Spirit spoke with tongues. Simon now saw power transferred to others. Hence he was determined to get this new power."

Saul (later Paul)

I only include the personal reference to the apostle Paul for the sake of completeness, as the term *"be filled with the Holy Spirit"* (Acts 9:17) is used. After Paul's encounter with Jesus on the road to Damascus, a disciple named Ananias had a vision to go to the house of Judas

on the street called Straight and lay hands on Paul that
he might receive his sight. The record states that at that
point Paul was already praying (verse 11), so perhaps in
his three days of blindness (verse 9) he had made his peace
with God and became a Christian, and this was why Ananias
called him "brother Saul."

"*17So Ananias departed and entered the house. And
laying his hands on him he said, 'Brother Saul, the Lord
Jesus who appeared to you on the road by which you
came has sent me so that you may regain your sight and
be filled with the Holy Spirit.' 18And immediately something like scales fell from his eyes, and he regained his
sight. Then he rose and was baptized; 19and taking food,
he was strengthened"* (Acts 9:17-19a).

There is no mention of speaking in tongues in this
passage. The statement by Ananias, *"and be filled with
the Holy Spirit"* was not in God's instructions in verse 12
and there appears to be no variant manuscripts of the
Greek there. Saul immediately regained his sight, then rose
and was baptized. The assumption is he was baptized in
water, followed by a public testimony to his faith in the
Son of God (verse 20).

However, we do know from Paul's own writings that
at some time (maybe at this time) he received the gift of
the Holy Spirit and began to speak in tongues. *"I thank
God that I speak in tongues more than all of you"* (I
Corinthians 14:18). He was not ashamed for it to be publicly
known.

The house of Cornelius

*"1At Caesarea there was a man named Cornelius, a
centurion of what was known as the Italian Cohort, 2a*

devout man who feared God with all his household, gave alms generously to the people, and prayed continually to God" (Acts 10:1-2). And so we are introduced to Cornelius. About the ninth hour, a Jewish time of prayer, this Italian had a vision of an angel of God. Part of the message from the angel was to send men to Joppa and bring back Peter, which he did. The next day, while Peter also was having a vision, *"¹⁹the Spirit said to him, Behold, three men are looking for you. ²⁰Rise and go down and accompany them without hesitation, for I have sent them'"* (Acts 10:19-20). So the next day Peter, with six of the brothers from Joppa (Acts 11:12), went with the men back to Cornelius.

"²⁴And on the following day they entered Caesarea. Cornelius was expecting them and had called together his relatives and close friends. ²⁵When Peter entered, Cornelius met him and fell down at his feet and worshiped him. ²⁶But Peter lifted him up, saying, 'Stand up; I too am a man'" (verses 24-26). After exchanging reports on their respective visions, Peter began sharing the news of the life of Christ, followed by his death and resurrection.

"⁴³'To him all the prophets bear witness that everyone who believes in him receives forgiveness of sins through his name.' ⁴⁴While Peter was still saying these things, the Holy Spirit fell on all who heard the word. ⁴⁵And the believers from among the circumcised who had come with Peter were amazed, because the gift of the Holy Spirit was poured out even on the Gentiles. ⁴⁶For they were hearing them speaking in tongues and extolling God" (verses 43-46).

Some call this the Gentile Pentecost because there was the miraculous outpouring of the Spirit as on the Day of Pentecost. God, by a sovereign act, "poured out" the Holy

Spirit to all who were gathered in the room. The record does not say whether others recognized the languages or not, and since the family of Cornelius and those he invited to hear Peter all understood the sermon, there was no need for the tongues to be recognized or understood.

Later, Peter had to explain his actions to the rest of the Twelve who were in Jerusalem and recount how he was led by a vision to speak to Gentiles, and how they interrupted his preaching by speaking in tongues as the Holy Spirit was being poured out. *"¹⁷If then God gave the same gift to them as he gave to us when we believed in the Lord Jesus Christ, who was I that I could stand in God's way?' ¹⁸When they heard these things they fell silent. And they glorified God, saying, 'Then to the Gentiles also God has granted repentance that leads to life'"* (Acts 11:17-18). We would be wise not to "stand in God's way" when He wants to specifically bless others in a way we're not expecting.

The church at Ephesus

Some years later, Paul was on his third missionary journey and came to Ephesus. *"¹There he found some disciples. ²And he said to them, 'Did you receive the Holy Spirit when you believed? And they said, 'No, we have not even heard that there is a Holy Spirit.' ³And he said, 'Into what then were you baptized?' They said, 'Into John's baptism.' ⁴And Paul said, 'John baptized with the baptism of repentance, telling the people to believe in the one who was to come after him, that is, Jesus.' ⁵On hearing this, they were baptized in the name of the Lord Jesus. ⁶And when Paul had laid his hands on them, the Holy Spirit came on them, and they began speaking in tongues and prophesying. ⁷There were about twelve men in all"* (Acts 19:1-7).

On this occasion, Paul found spiritually hungry people who quickly believed his report. Paul, now recognized as an apostle though not one of the Twelve who witnessed the resurrection of Jesus, simply laid his hands on the 12 men, *"and they began speaking in tongues and prophesying."* And it remains just as simple today to receive the gift of the Holy Spirit, either by you asking God, or by laying on of hands.

19
Getting the Right Emphasis

When I published the 24-page booklet *So You Want to Speak in Tongues* in 1978, I should have known better. It was not because it was lacking powerful teaching, because I still believe what I wrote to this day, 40 years later. It was because I had the cart before the horse in the title! It was a catchy title and had a catchy subtitle: "For those who have quit fighting and started longing."

Yet nowhere in the Gospels or the book of Acts were believers encouraged to *want* to speak in tongues. We have already seen in chapter 2 of this book that even in the promises of Jesus to his disciples concerning the gift of the Holy Spirit, he did not mention speaking in tongues (Luke 24:49; John 7:39, Acts 1:4-5 and Acts 1:8).

Even Peter in his first sermon in Acts chapter 2 answered his listener's question of *"What shall we do?"* (verse 37) by saying, *"Repent and be baptized every one of you in the name of Jesus Christ for the forgiveness of your sins, and you will receive the gift of the Holy Spirit"* (verse 38). Note the "receive" but no "want" or "desire" for speaking in tongues. It was not until Acts 10:46 that the phrase "speaking in tongues" occurs again after Acts 2:4, and this as a comment on "the gift of the Holy Spirit" that was poured out in the house of Cornelius (verses 44,45). Peter had not mentioned tongues at all in his sermon. As the Mirror Bible paraphrases I Corinthians 13:1 so aptly, *"Speaking in tongues is not the point; love is."*

What is of interest about "how to receive the gift" is to notice that in Peter's sermon the emphasis is first on repentance of sins to obtain forgiveness (which precedes salvation) and then *"you will receive the gift."* Yes, I've known of people who say you can skip the repentance and speak in tongues. But that is not the biblical order. You must be saved, and if you are taught correctly the next minute you could receive the Holy Spirit in all his fullness by exercising your faith.

The point I am taking time to make is that the biblical evidence is for a believer is to seek to know God better and fuller, and be available for anything and everything God has for them. Then they are ready to receive by faith the "gift of the Holy Spirit" from God. Upon receiving the gift they will have the ability to use God's power, which is then manifested in speaking in tongues: *"But you will receive power when the Holy Spirit has come upon you"* (Acts 1:8) and speaking in tongues will flow from that power as a physical confirmation of that spiritual event.

Any seeking is to be for the fulness of the Holy Spirit in your life, and the powerful benefits will then flow from the Spirit within. A good example of why we need the Holy Spirit is given when Jesus said, *"He will glorify me, for he will take what is mine and declare it to you"* (John 16:14). So to know better the ways and will of God, the

Holy Spirit will reveal them to a hungry believer. To apply this to receiving the gift of the Holy Spirit, seek a deeper, fuller relationship with your heavenly Father, and when you want that more than anything else, ask for the gift and speaking in tongues will come with the package. Get the order right and you will get the manifestations in their rightful place in your life and in the church life.

The Mirror Bible gives an excellent paraphrase of I Corinthians 14:12: *"Let me make it very clear, while speaking in tongues has its personal benefits, do not make it the thing everybody wants to do! Then you miss the whole point of spiritual gifts! ... The greater blessing is not in getting the blessing but in being a blessing to others."* Again, the emphasis should not be to want the manifestation of tongues but to want to "edify one another" (Romans 14:19) and receiving the power from on high will do that in so many different ways.

An event in the book of Acts that illustrates what happens when the order is reversed. In chapter 8, Simon the sorcerer saw the apostles laying hands on people who then received the gift and spoke in tongues. *"[18]Now when Simon saw that the Spirit was given through the laying on of the apostles' hands, he offered them money, [19]saying, 'Give me this power also, so that anyone on whom I lay my hands may receive the Holy Spirit'"* (Acts 8:18-19). He received an immediate rebuke from Peter: *"[20]But Peter said to him, 'May your silver perish with you, because you thought you could obtain the gift of God with money! [21]You have neither part nor lot in this matter, for your heart is not right before God. [22]Repent, therefore, of this wickedness of yours, and pray to the Lord that, if possible, the intent of your heart may be forgiven you"* (Acts 8:20-22).

Albert Barnes writes in his commentary: "We have 'nothing' which we can present for his favors. And yet there are many who seek to 'purchase' the favor of God. Some do it by alms and prayers; some by penance and fasting; some by attempting to make their own hearts better, and by self-righteousness; and some by penitence and tears. All these will not 'purchase' his favor.'"

Paul in his letter of I Corinthians was writing to a church that we could safely assume had a majority of tongues-speaking Christians (I Corinthians 14:23). Paul is not concerned with receiving the gift but with how to use it, so he told them: *"Now I want you all to speak in tongues, but even more to prophesy"* (14:5a). Why? Because everyone could understand prophecy in their everyday language and therefore be built up by the word of God for the moment or the future (14:5b-20).

"¹⁸I thank God that I speak in tongues more than all of you (emphasising the constancy of usage of the God-given ability in his life), *¹⁹Nevertheless, in church I would rather speak five words with my mind in order to instruct others, than ten thousand words in a tongue"* (I Corinthians 14:18-19). Then he told them later, *"do not forbid speaking in tongues"* (verse 39).

I Corinthians chapters 12 to 14 teaches the use and position of speaking in tongues in our private and church life, and should be read and studied after you have received the gift.

20

How to Receive and Activate the Gift

This is what I suggest that you do. First, simply sit down quietly somewhere; you don't have to kneel, you don't have to light candles or raise your hands to heaven, and you don't need other believers encouraging you. Just sit quietly somewhere and follow God's instruction to *"Be still, and know that I am God"* (Psalm 46:10). Now remember, you do not need to stir up your emotions, you do not need to breathe in and out deeply. Just sit quietly in God's presence and stay your mind on Him.

Many of God's promises are **voice-activated**, and the gift of the Holy Spirit with speaking in tongues is one of those. If you have faith in some truth, you will prove it by speaking out. I repeat, the gift of the Holy Spirit is received by a faith action.

If you feel it would help you, quietly thank the Father for the great, beautiful gift of eternal life that you have within you, for Christ who now lives in you (Galatians 2:20). You might tell God you are ready to accept "the gift of the Holy Spirit" in all its fulness. *"If you then,*

*who are evil, know how to give good gifts to your children,
how much more will the heavenly Father give the Holy
Spirit to those who ask him!"* (Luke 11:13)

Then stop praying and immediately speak out, clearly
and distinctly, the first syllables that come to your mind.
Just speak them out, however strange they may sound,
and keep on speaking. God will not let you down; He is
giving you the words to utter. And that's it—no stress, no
strain, no pain. You are speaking out the words God is
giving you to utter—quietly and confidently operating the
manifestation of speaking in tongues.

Keep on speaking in tongues for a few minutes, and
then stop and rejoice! Could it be this simple? Yes! It doesn't
take a half-night of prayer, it doesn't take any pleading
and agonizing before a "reluctant" God; it probably takes
less just a few minutes. This is just part of the "power"
(Acts 1:8) you receive when you are "clothed with" the
Holy Spirit in your life.

Now, by an act of your will, start speaking in tongues
again. Let it flow forth because you are speaking the wonderful
works of God (Acts 2:11), you are magnifying God (Acts
10:46), you are speaking divine secrets to God (I Corinthians
14:2). And now, do not be surprised if the thrill of what
is happening starts to show itself in your emotions. Now
is the time to get emotional, not before you speak in tongues.
You have a right to be excited for you are bringing forth
a manifestation of the spirit specifically designed to profit
you as you fellowship with and worship your wonderful
and loving Father.

Speaking in tongues is not just an experience for one
occasion, it is a God-given ability that can be exercised

daily to bring forth profit. Determine to speak in tongues every day as part of your private devotional time.

The moment you will to speak forth, God will have the words ready for you to utter. He will not fail you— every time you will to speak, God will energize that act by giving you words in an unknown language, words of praise and prayer to *"praise the Lord for his goodness, and his wonderful works to the children of men!"* (Psalm 107:8). Now you can praise God with perfect praise as you operate the manifestation of speaking in tongues. Go back and read the above paragraphs again.

Further explanation of speaking in tongues

So often it is claimed that these manifestations are "100% supernatural." This might sound spiritual, but it cannot be backed up by the Word. There are hundreds of examples that show the principle that God always works in co-operation with humans, and that humans make the first move. I have been told that this is not how the apostles received in the book of Acts—but it is! Examine the record again.

"And they were all filled with the Holy Spirit and began to speak in other tongues as the Spirit gave them utterance" (Acts 2:4). *"They were all filled* [God did the filling]... *and* [the apostles used the mechanics of speech and] *began to speak..."* It was not the Holy Spirit who began to speak; it was the apostles. If God took over their vocal chords, then He overstepped man's free will. Since God has not done this anywhere else in the Word in His relationship with humans, then I fail to see why He would do it here.

Also, I would remind you of the instructions in I Corinthians chapter 14 as to when to speak in tongues and when to keep silent. *"27If any speak in a tongue, let there be only two or at most three, and each in turn, and let someone interpret. 28But if there is no one to interpret, let each of them keep silent in church and speak to himself and to God"* (I Corinthians 14:27-28). Surely God would know the right time; yet such instruction is necessary for it is humans who do the speaking. It is far safer and simpler to believe the integrity of the Word that says: *"They were all filled... and [they] began to speak..."*

The mechanics of speaking in tongues involve the same functions as when you speak in your native language. Say "Praise the Lord" out aloud, and notice what happened. Your lips moved, your tongue moved, you "projected" the sound from your vocal chords—these things are the mechanics of speech. "The exhaled air provides the controlled production of speech sounds." When the apostles "began to speak" they too had to move their lips, their tongues, and vibrated their vocal chords. **They** did the speaking.

Now there is one difference between speaking in tongues and when you said "Praise the Lord" a few moments ago. I may have suggested the words to you, but it was an act of your will for your mind to formulate the words "Praise the Lord" on your lips. When you speak in tongues, it is God who gives you the words to say. Notice the second part of Acts 2:4: "... [they] began to speak in tongues, as the Spirit gave them utterance" (KJV). Let me share some other translations: *"...according as the Spirit gave them words to utter"* (Weymouth)," *"...as the Spirit enabled them to express themselves"* (Moffatt). Vincent's Word Studies makes this comment: "Kept giving them the language and the appropriate words as the case required from time to time... Utterance. Used only by Luke and in Acts. Literally, to utter." God gives the words to utter; you do the speaking.

Now it should be fairly obvious that you cannot speak in English and in tongues at the same moment. There is no need for believers to first make any statement in English whatsoever. All that is needed to speak in tongues is an act of the believer's will to do it! The necessary power is already resident, the ability is already there; and God is going to give the words to utter—not in your native language, but in a language unknown to you, the believer. Without you, He will not; without Him, you cannot.

Remember John 7:38: *"Out of his heart [from deep within, CSB] will flow rivers of living water."* It is not a gift to be received from without, but a manifestation of that which is already within. When you will to act, by moving your lips, your tongue, your vocal chords, a miracle will take place in a split-second. God will give the words to utter to your spirit, your spirit will give them to your mind, and your mind will put them "on the tip of your tongue" as it were. This will happen so fast that you will not be conscious of the process; you will simply speak out those odd-sounding syllables that do literally seem to be on the tip of your tongue. You do the speaking; God gives the words to utter—and when you just keep speaking it out, it will flow like rivers of living water.

Even though I am writing about the mechanics of speaking in tongues, I do not want to suggest that this is possible without believing faith. I fully acknowledge that I am dealing here with a *"manifestation of the spirit"* (I Corinthians 12:7) and some may feel that dwelling upon the mechanics is such a cold way of co-operating with God in such a beautiful and profitable manifestation. There is a place for believing faith—but it is not believing that God will grasp your jaw and move it up and down, then wiggle your tongue, and produce vibrations in your vocal chords. You have the natural ability to do this at any time you so will. Why should God have to do it for you? And why should He break the principle of the free will of man to get you to show forth what He has already given within?

The place of believing faith is simply this: you are to believe that the syllables you speak forth are from the Father and are words of praise, thanksgiving, prayer and blessing directed to Him. The point of believing, then, is the moment before you speak out the first syllable. God will not let you be ashamed or embarrassed (Romans 10:11), He will not give you a worthless stone when you need life-building bread (Luke 11:11). Have confidence in Him (I John 5:14-15), and you will have what you desire. It takes believing faith to show forth the spirit, an action, so open your mouth and speak it forth for the glory of God.

Let the rivers flow

Let me summarize what I have shared in this book about one of the nine beautiful manifestations of the Holy Spirit—speaking in tongues. I have quoted earlier from John 7:37b-39: *"37If anyone thirsts, let him come to me and drink. 38Whoever believes in me, as the Scripture has said, 'Out of his heart [his innermost being] will flow rivers of living water.' 39Now this he said about the Spirit, whom those who believed in him were to receive, for as yet the Spirit had not been given, because Jesus was not yet glorified."*

It is made quite clear that *"the rivers of living water"* which shall flow is a word picture for a spiritual experience. The important word in the phrase is the verb "to flow." The stronger word "gush" is used by some scholars, giving the picture of a spring or a fountain.

Verse 39 indicates that God's gift was to become available on the Day of Pentecost, *"Now this he said about the Spirit, whom those who believed in him were to receive..."* The word "receive" is the word *lambano*, and means to receive objectively, to be evident, to receive into manifestation. All who believed, from Acts 2:4 onwards, have the ability to show forth into evidence the spoken "rivers of living water" by means of speaking in tongues.

The word picture of the river of living water brings to mind two truths regarding speaking in tongues. The first is that the flow is not a trickle—a word here, a word there. It is a fluent speaking forth, in just the same way as the native of any country speaks his own language. I believe we should not accept anything less than a flowing language as a manifestation of speaking in tongues.

The second truth is a reinforcement of what we learn from I Corinthians chapters 14-16, that speaking in tongues will always produce profit. Wherever the life-giving waters flow, there is growth. *"The one who speaks in a tongue builds up himself"* (I Corinthians 14:4). The right usage of the manifestation of speaking in tongues in the believer's devotional life will bring spiritual growth and depth to the believer. Speaking in tongues is certainly not the "be-all and end-all" of Christian life. But it is a provision of a loving Father for the profit of His children, and I have endeavored to share some of the ways that this profit is evident.

Last Words

This has been an exciting book to write. I have carefully gone over the text, immersed myself in the events, and presented the result to you as clearly yet accurately as I could. I have read favorite verses that have blessed me over many years, and the thrill of seeing the impact of them on the events has not dimmed. I've read other verses that have led me up interesting trails through the historic events and added to my understanding of how it must have been to the Apostles and other believers.

I trust that you have touched by those exciting days also, and that the journey has been a catalyst to your own amazement at how God used mostly "unlearned and ignorant" people to steer the church in its early years. His church has already lasted for over 20 centuries, despite constant opposition. Some of what you have read about is still in evidence today; other "signs and wonders" may or may not be seen again. One thing is certain: if you will read this book again you will be surprised at how much you missed first time around!

I have kept the book as an journey of exploration and inspiration and not a commentary, the same as I did with the books *I'm Excited About Ephesians, I'm Excited About Colossians* and *Exploring the Mission Statement of Jesus.* There are, however, many truths that relate to the historical record and various church practices that you might be inspired to follow up in some depth.

Here are a few such matters: What is the difference between the Old Testament pattern, where the Holy Spirit "came upon" people, to the Gospels where the Holy Spirit "abides" with believers, to post-Pentecost in the book of Acts and the epistles, where the Holy Spirit is "in" a person? What is the difference between having the Holy Spirit abiding with you compared to being "filled with the Holy Spirit?" Why were only two people in the Gospels "filled?" Was the Holy Spirit working on your life before you became a Christian? Does a Christian who does not speak in tongues have the Holy Spirit?

While I have described the various ways the "power from on high" was displayed and used in the book of Acts, the manifestations and gifts listed in I Corinthians chapters 12 to 14 and in other letters is best left to a separate volume. Even a quick reading of those chapters reveals that the operation of the "gift of the Holy Spirit" is controlled by the believer, who should abide by the inspired statements.

Finally, do not let the blessing of God's Word die on your hands. Share these truths with your family and friends. Start a stream of blessing in your church or fellowship by giving out copies of this book, for *"it is more blessed to give than to receive"* (Acts 20:35). Watch the reactions and you will be filled with joy at having a part of this ministry of God's positive Word.

If you have been helped by this book, please leave a comment on our website or the website where you purchased the book. Write while the thrill is upon you. Do it today.

www.PeterWade.com

My thanks to...

Vivien Wade, who has shared in my ministry for over 60 years and who faithfully keeps me going;

Irene Baroni for her great editorial services, who always makes me look good as if I know American English like the back of my hand, and whose gentle editing and perceptive insights have vastly improved this work;

Brian Trenhaile for his content advice at my request;

John Crouch for his Greek language advice, confirming my understanding;

Kevin Bell for his reading an advance copy and his glowing assessment;

And finanacial supporters of this ministry worldwide who have made the production of this book possible.

Bible Acknowledgements

Scripture quotations marked AMP are from the *Amplified® Bible,* Copyright © 1954, 1958, 1962, 1964, 1965, 1987 by The Lockman Foundation. Used by permission.

Scripture quotations marked ASV are from the *American Standard Version,* 1929. Public domain.

Scripture quotations marked CEV are from the *Contemporary English Version,* Copyright © 1991 by American Bible Society. All rights reserved. Used by permission.

Scripture quotations marked CLV are from the *Concordant Literal New Testament,* Copyright © 1976 by Concordant Publishing Concern. Used by permission.

Scripture quotations marked CSB are taken from the *Holman Christian Standard Bible®,*Copyright © 1999-2009 by Holman Bible Publishers. Used by permission.

Scripture quotations marked ESV are taken from *The Holy Bible, English Standard Version®* (ESV). Copyright © 2007 by Crossway, a publishing ministry of Good News Publishers. Used by permission. All rights reserved.

Scripture quotations marked GNB are taken from the *Good News Bible,* Copyright © 1976 by American Bible Society. Used by permission.

Scripture quotations marked KJV are from the *King James Version.* Public domain.

Scripture quotations marked Mirror are from the *Mirror Bible,* Copyright © 2012 by Francois du Toit. All rights reserved. Used by permission.

Scripture quotations marked Moffatt are from *The Bible. A New Translation,* James Moffatt, Copyright © 1954 by James A.R. Moffatt. All rights reserved. Used by permission.

Scripture quotations marked MSG are from *The Message,* Copyright © 2002, by Eugene H. Peterson. Used by permission of NavPress Publishing Group.

About the Author

PETER AND VIVIEN WADE have ministered together since 1958 and continue to do so decades later. After graduating from Bible College together, they served pastorates in Australia, and for the past 50 years have fulfilled a Bible teaching ministry in the United States and Australia, and worldwide on the Internet since 1995 (www.PeterWade.com). Peter is the author of many books and audio and video teachings, and Vivien is the author of two books of poems.

Peter and Vivien are co-founders of Positive Word Ministries Inc., a trans-denominational teaching ministry, and Peter is the president. They make their home in metropolitan Adelaide, South Australia.

Printed in Great Britain
by Amazon